A Decade of D&H

AF477345

By Karl R. Zimmermann

with additional photographs by Roger Cook and others.

 Published by Delford Press, Post Office Box 27, Oradell, N. J. 07649.
ISBN 0-931726-02-6

For Jennifer and Emily, who like trains too.

Acknowledgements

Among the many individuals who have helped with *A Decade of D&H*, two made truly monumental contributions. About half a hundred of the photographs in the pages that follow carry Roger Cook's credit; without them, the illustration would be infinitely inferior in both breadth and artistry. Furthermore, Mr. Cook has worked with me throughout the book's composition—supplying information, making suggestions, providing encouragement.

Bob Mohowski has generously shared a wealth of ideas, information, and materials on the D&H. The situation report on pages 62-63 is largely his in both conception and execution, and a number of his photographs appear in the book as well. Therefore, my very special thanks go to Messrs. Cook and Mohowski, without whose various contributions this volume would be much the poorer.

Other excellent photographers have kindly shared their work: Tom and George Kelcec, Steve Ward, Max Robin, and George Berisso. My thanks to all. Robert Gordon, for twenty years my literary mentor and frequent editor, once again has done his best to eliminate the excesses and inaccuracies of my prose. As always, I am grateful. For the book's front cover design, my thanks to Michael Tobin and Kay Ritta of Ritta Design.

Over the years, I have met with unfailing hospitality at the D&H. While president, Bruce Sterzing gave me much of his valuable time on a number of occasions to help me better understand the railroad and his vision for it. Carl Belke, Jim Champlin, Jim Colpoys, Marv Davis, Gene Gilchrist, Howard Hontz, the late Matt Levins, Richard Long, Becky Macumber, Gus Negus, Tony Steele, and Dick Williams are among the others at the D&H who have helped. I deeply appreciate their courtesy and assistance—and that of any others I may have neglected to name.

Though the bulk of the research for this book was done directly at the D&H, two literary sources deserve mention. Jim Shaughnessy's excellent *Delaware & Hudson* (Howell-North Books: 1967) covers the railroad to the era where *A Decade of D&H* begins and thus was an essential source of information on the road's early history. Also, *Trains* Magazine was frequently useful as it chronicled, both in news items and short features, the ups and downs of D&H in the turbulent ten years just completed.

To write even so brief a book as this takes a great deal of time—time that must be carved from here and there, always at the expense of other things. For understanding this and helping in very many ways, I thank Laurel, my wife. Finally, I can't reiterate too often my appreciation of the continuing support, encouragement, and assistance received from my parents.

Karl R. Zimmermann

Englewood, New Jersey
April 1978

FRONT COVER: The PA's on a "Penn Division Special" northbound near Starrucca, Pa., on October 19, 1974. KARL R. ZIMMERMANN

BACK COVER: A cold winter's evening at Fort Edward, N.Y. ROGER COOK

TITLE PAGE: No. 604 leads an eastbound at Cobleskill, N.Y. ROGER COOK

FACING PAGE: Bending the iron for the Sharks at the south end of the yard at Whitehall, N.Y., in March 1975. KARL R. ZIMMERMANN

ABOVE: Also at Whitehall, a U23B burrows in snow. ROGER COOK

Occasionally the casual hand of chance lends an uncharacteristic neatness to history. Such has been the case on the Delaware & Hudson Railway, where a decade has recently concluded that was as perfect in its proportions as it was rich in interesting activity. On August 1, 1967, Frederick C. "Buck" Dumaine, Jr., a staunch individualist, had taken over as president and chief executive officer of the D&H. On August 1, 1977, ten years later to the day, Carl B. Sterzing, Jr., another individualist, resigned those same posts under fire.

The intervening decade had seen much of interest happen on the D&H. No fewer than eight new classes of motive power were added to the roster, from such exotica as Alco-GE PA's and Baldwin "Sharknoses" to substantial numbers of Electro-Motive Division GP38-2's and GP39-2's, which have begun a new era in D&H motive-power acquisition. Long-haul D&H passenger trains made news three times: when *The Laurentian* was reequipped in 1967, discontinued at Amtrak's inception in 1971, and, after a three-year hiatus, reborn as *The Adirondack.*

During this busy decade, the D&H celebrated its 150th birthday with much festivity, including an Albany-to-Montreal round-trip excursion with double-headed steam locomotives and a display train of D&H artifacts that toured the system behind a pair of PA's. The railroad became part of the Norfolk & Western, through Dereco, an N&W holding company, but did not become part of Conrail. Instead, the D&H nearly doubled in size at the time of Conrail's formation, from a modest 747 route-miles to approximately 1400. This decade, 1967-1977, was not an easy one for D&H, but the road operated in the black for five of those years, largely through belt-tightening and hard work at all levels. It also operated with considerable style, for such was the penchant of the men at the top.

The Delaware & Hudson Railroad found 1967 an especially crucial year. It was then that Dumaine took over as president and CEO. (He had been chairman of the board since December 1966.) Though he wasn't to remain long, he left his mark, particularly on D&H passenger service. Furthermore, that year saw a significant change in the direction of D&H motive power policy, as a long-term allegiance to Alco was overridden by the purchase of diesels from General Electric and General Motors Electro-Motive Division. Also in 1967, the United States Supreme Court and the Interstate Commerce Commission laid the groundwork—in decisions relative to the Penn Central merger and Norfolk & Western responsibility for the D&H and other lines—upon which the future of the Delaware & Hudson would be based.

Dumaine's brief presidency will be remembered primarily for two things. First, it was he who in the late fall of 1967 bought four Alco PA1's for the D&H and gave them the chance to become the world's most famous diesel locomotives. Second, he made a stand for independence for the Delaware & Hudson vis-à-vis the Norfolk & Western. This issue of independence, though in its original terms quickly resolved against Dumaine's position, would continue to burn through the next ten years, albeit with other specifics and definitions. In 1977, the question of "independence" was to lead to the departure of another D&H president; in 1968 it led to Dumaine's.

The first news of the Dumaine presidency was good, however, particularly for railroad enthusiasts. Dumaine was known as a passenger-oriented railroader, and he proved this once again shortly after taking over the D&H. He had been president of the New Haven from 1951 to 1954 (when he lost a proxy fight to Patrick McGinnis), and during those years added passenger-train miles to NYNH&H timetables, though nationwide they were being reduced. By the time Dumaine came to the D&H, this trend toward discontinuance of passenger service across the United States had gained the momentum of a runaway. In 1951, passenger-miles in the country totaled 34.6 billion; by 1967 this figure had shrunk to 15.2 bil-

Running northbound at Dresden Station, N.Y., during its last winter, The Laurentian *is a handsome and substantial consist, with back-to-back PA's trailing a baggage mail, diner-lounge, and four coaches.* KARL R. ZIMMERMANN

lion, considerably less than half; by 1970, the eve of Amtrak, it would shrink further, to 10.8 billion.

In 1967, these items were news in the larger world of the passenger train. The pro-passenger Burlington Route eliminated the *Texas Zephyr*. Monon dropped the *Thoroughbred* and became freight-only. Northern Pacific asked to drop the *Mainstreeter* and Southern Pacific the *Lark* and *Golden State*. Santa Fe, by all odds the railroad with the most intense commitment to passenger service of any, posted for discontinuance all of its secondary trains, including the famous *Chief*.

During the previous year, the trains which had competed with the D&H for New York City-Montreal business—the daylight *Ambassador* and overnight *Montrealer/Washingtonian,* on the Canadian National-Central Vermont-Boston & Maine-New Haven route—had been eliminated. Also discontinued in 1966 were the Erie Lackawanna's *Phoebe Snow* and the Denver & Rio Grande Western's *Royal Gorge* remnant and *Prospector*. These EL and D&RGW discontinuances were to bear on the D&H passenger story, as rolling stock thus made surplus eventually arrived on D&H property.

December 3, 1967, was a particularly bleak day for the Northeast's passenger train faithful, for the New York Central's *20th Century Limited,* the most famous train in the land, came to an end. By this date, however, the Central's near neighbor D&H had been committed by Dumaine to a very different course of action. Already the road's two passenger trains—the New York-Montreal *Laurentian* and *Montreal Limited,* which had shared with the *Century* the 142-mile run from Albany south along the Hudson River—were receiving new cars. And by mid-December, new locomotives for these trains would also arrive at the D&H's Colonie Shops, a few miles north of Albany.

Prior to Dumaine's coming, the D&H's stance on passenger trains had been as negative as its neighbors'. Under William White (president from 1954 to 1966), D&H tried to drop the daylight *Laurentian,* in 1963; the Interstate Commerce Commission said no. Later, management attempted to eliminate the diners and downgrade the train through the introduction of leased rail diesel cars, but New York State intervened to block this move.

Laurentian *scenes during the train's final year: At Lacolle, P.Q. (top). Facing page: At Cooperville, N.Y., in summer (top left) and winter (bottom); the crew boarding at Rouses Point, N.Y. (top right).* KARL R. ZIMMERMANN

Bottom left: Frederick C. "Buck" Dumaine. FABIAN BACHRACH

19
16

Facing page: Wearing heavy gloves against the bitter cold, a D&H trainman watches from the Dutch door of a PC coach at Whitehall. Just ahead in this Laurentian *consist is an ACF coach dating from 1939; designer Raymond Loewy is responsible for the distinctive porthole.* STEVEN WARD

Above: In December of 1968, The Laurentian *runs north on the Saratoga Division. In the consist are a Loewy-styled ACF coach and a New York Central parlor car—the latter soon to be removed from* Laurentian *service. Left: PA's Nos. 18 and 17 have been fueled and are about to leave Whitehall with a short consist.*
KARL R. ZIMMERMANN

DELAWARE
AND
HUDSON

NEW YORK
SARATOGA SPRINGS
ADIRONDACKS
LAKE CHAMPLAIN
FORT TICONDEROGA
PLATTSBURGH
MONTREAL

Local Time

Passenger Train Schedules
EFFECTIVE JUNE 14, 1970

Route of the Famous
MONTREAL LIMITED
Between New York and Montreal

Nos. 34 and 35, The Laurentians, *meet at Whitehall in freezing rain (top); soon, No. 34 departs southbound (bottom).* KARL R. ZIMMERMANN

Singing quite a different song, Buck Dumaine, in the second month of his presidency, told a National Railway Historical Society group that "You don't make money by pulling off trains." That was September 1967. In October, he bought a dozen passenger cars from the Denver & Rio Grande Western, cars which had been used on the *Royal Gorge* and, particularly, the *Prospector*. All built by Pullman-Standard, they comprised three baggage-mail, one baggage, five 52-seat coaches, two diner-lounges, and a buffet lounge. He also bought, from the Santa Fe, four Alco PA's, which before long would become the last of their kind.

All this equipment was repainted at Colonie Shops into D&H blue and yellow, set off against stainless steel—flat sheeting on the flanks of the PA's and fluted siding on the passenger cars. On December 26, about three weeks after the *Century's* demise, the first PA-powered *Laurentian* rolled north. Suddenly, railroad enthusiasts in the Northeast, who had recently been buffeted by mostly bad news, turned their attention to these bright-looking passenger trains —and to the entire D&H as well.

What they found—in addition to PA's and streamliners—was this: a diverse diesel fleet that had just recently admitted non-Alco members in the form of GE U30C's and EMD SD45's; a colorful and intricate paint scheme on all the locomotives, in an era of increasingly dull and simplified liveries; a railroad large enough to be interesting yet small enough to know intimately, the antithesis of the about-to-be-formed Penn Central; a route replete with grand scenery—most notably but by no means exclusively on the Champlain Subdivision, which plays tag with the west shore of that lake for much of the way from Whitehall to Rouses Point, N. Y.—and operating challenges, particularly over the Pennsylvania Subdivision's Ararat grade and the Susquehanna Subdivision's Richmondville Hill and Belden Hill.

In 1967 D&H was, in route and basic operations, much what it had been thirty years earlier, in the mid-30's, after it had faced the need to alter its character and had done so. The D&H has its roots in the Delaware & Hudson Canal Company, which was incorporated in 1823, making it the oldest transportation company in the United States. The canal was dug from Honesdale, Pa., to Rond-

Sun, snow, and PA's Nos. 18 and 17 leading the southbound Laurentian *along the shore of a frozen Lake Champlain at Port Henry, N. Y.* KARL R. ZIMMERMANN

Above: The Laurentian *breezes into the picturesque depot at Westport, N.Y. Facing page: It's January 2, 1970, and after a week of annulments due to snow, cold, and lack of motive power, the* Montreal Limited *arrives hours late at Rouses Point behind E8's Nos. 822 and 815—leased from Dereco partner Erie Lackawanna and making their initial run. After the southbound* Laurentian *comes and goes, the E8's are run forward for fueling and watering. The RS3 is a switcher.* ROGER COOK

out, N. Y., near Kingston on the Hudson River, a distance of 108 miles. Its purpose: to move anthracite coal from Pennsylvania's Lackawanna Valley to New York City.

For the first sixteen miles—from the mines at Carbondale to the canal at Honesdale—the coal traveled over the D&H's "Gravity Railroad," an operation powered by cables and stationary steam engines. When, in the early 1870's, the D&H Canal Company moved into railroading as we know it today, the cargo of overwhelming importance was still coal, and it was to remain so for many years. By the 1930's, however, anthracite was declining rapidly as a home-heating fuel and the D&H, after a century of dependence on coal-hauling, had to develop new competences.

The D&H became "The Bridge Line to New England and Canada," both in slogan and fact, making a business of the high-speed forwarding of "overhead" traffic between connections—a necessary rededication which thirty years later, in the merger-prone '60's, was to leave the railroad vulnerable. Since the demise of anthracite, the D&H has generated or terminated on-line a relatively small percentage of its traffic; more than most roads, it is heavily dependent on its connections.

The heart of the D&H, over which most trains pass, was the Susquehanna Division (now called the Susquehanna *Sub*division), which extends from Binghamton, N. Y., on the west to Mechanicville, N. Y., on the east, with a secondary route branching off at Delanson for Albany. From Nineveh Junction, 24 miles northeast of Binghamton, the Pennsylvania Subdivision probes south over Ararat to Carbondale, Scranton, and Wilkes-Barre—anthracite country. North from Albany and Mechanicville runs the Saratoga Subdivision to Whitehall, at the foot of Lake Champlain; from there the Champlain Subdivision extends to Rouses Point, on the Canadian border. (Formerly considered divisions, these districts were demoted to subdivisions at the advent of Dereco.)

When Buck Dumaine took over the D&H in 1967, the railroad still had most of its traditional "friendly connections" intact. To the north, at Rouses Point, traffic went to the Napierville Junction Railway, a D&H subsidiary, and the Canadian National for points in eastern Canada. At Mechanicville was the all-important east-west interchange with the Boston & Maine for New England traffic. There were a number of connections with the Erie Lackawanna: at Binghamton, at Jefferson Junction, Pa. (on the D&H's "Penn Divi-

Facing page, top: In its last month of operation, The Laurentian *casts a near-perfect reflection at Chazy, N. Y.* ROGER COOK

Facing page, bottom: On this southbound Laurentian, *seen here at Comstock, N. Y., the PA's outnumber the coaches. Though largely excluded from the 1967 reequipping and therefore not as glamorous as* The Laurentian, *the overnight* Montreal Limited *was consistently better patronized than the day train. On this page, it's nearly 9:30 P.M. on a November night in 1970, and the* Montreal Limited *is about to leave Montreal's Windsor Station.* KARL R. ZIMMERMANN

Mail once played an important part in keeping passenger trains healthy, or at least alive. Above, the mail sacks are out on the platform for loading at Plattsburg, N. Y., as the southbound Laurentian *pulls in. Facing page: Sacks are piled in readiness on the baggage cart at Plattsburg (left); business is conducted despite the rain at Rouses Point (right).* ROGER COOK

PLATTSBURG
A R E

sion," and in the shadow of the Erie's Starrucca Viaduct), at Scranton, and at Plymouth Junction—near Wilkes-Barre, on the EL's Bloomsburg Branch.

Traffic was interchanged with the Lehigh Valley westbound at Sayre, Pa. (via pooled LV-D&H run-throughs from Binghamton on trackage rights over the EL to Owego, thence on the LV's Auburn Branch to Sayre), and west-, east-, and southbound at Wilkes-Barre. Interchange with the Central Railroad of New Jersey was there too. Also in the Wilkes-Barre area, westbound traffic for the Pennsylvania Railroad's Sunbury line was turned over at Buttonwood Yard, reached from the D&H yard at Hudson, Pa., via the Wilkes-Barre Connecting Railroad. At Glenville Junction (near Schenectady, N. Y.) and South Albany, cars were exchanged with the New York Central. At Rutland, Vt., were interchanges with the Green Mountain Railroad, the Vermont Railway, and the Clarendon & Pittsford.

Much of the D&H story of the next decade would involve these connections: how some deteriorated, and how the D&H tried to keep them active and strong. But Dumaine was not much involved

Top: Albany Union Station was in its death throes in October 1968 when the cook aboard The Laurentian's *diner-lounge* Mt. Timpanogos *chatted with friends under the station's umbrella sheds.* STEVEN WARD

Bottom: The Laurentian *changes from Alco to EMD power at Albany Union.* KARL R. ZIMMERMANN

Facing page: Alco Century No. 617—seen here as the Belden Hill pusher, running light between Port Crane and Sanitaria Springs, N. Y.—is every bit as powerful-looking and gutsy as Genesee's Belgian Roan horses (bottom). Other D&H six-axle power in the form of a pair of big U-boats works south on the Penn Division near Lanesboro, Pa. (top). ROGER COOK

617
GENESEE
BEER & ALE

Above: U30C No. 705 works east at Hillcrest on the Susquehanna Subdivision. Facing page: A westbound local freight behind RS36 No. 5016 meets an east-bound road freight led by C628's Nos. 607 and 611 between Bainbridge and Sidney, N. Y. (top); that same through freight is seen just west of Bainbridge (bottom). ROGER COOK

in this story, for soon after assuming the presidency of the D&H he took a stand for independence from the N&W—and lost. The formation of Penn Central—primarily responsible for the D&H's eventual interchange crises—also lay behind Dumaine's departure, though somewhat indirectly.

The tangled situation that came to a head in 1967 and was resolved in 1968 had been developing for years. When the Nickel Plate and Wabash were merged into the Norfolk & Western in 1964, the D&H (along with the Erie Lackawanna and the Boston & Maine) was granted the possibility of future inclusion in the system, though they were denied inclusion at that time. "Appendix O" of the ICC's ruling stipulated that, should their merger into N&W become equitable to all parties, D&H-EL-B&M could re-petition for this at any time in the next five years. And when the Penn Central merger—already half-a-dozen years in the making—was postponed yet again in March 1967 by the Supreme Court, this delay was to assure indemnity for D&H-EL-B&M.

In June 1967, the ICC ordered the N&W to take in these three roads by July 17, thus allowing the PC merger to proceed. Neither D&H nor N&W was pleased with the specifics, and eventually the ICC revised its order and changed the terms of the assumption to ones both railroads could accept. Thus it was that on February 1, 1968, at long last, Penn Central became a reality. The EL came under the N&W umbrella on April 1, 1968, and the D&H followed on July 1. B&M stayed out.

The arrangement as finally hammered out worked this way. The railroad assets of the D&H were sold to Dereco, Inc., an N&W-controlled holding company which also embraced the EL, but assumed full responsibility for the debts of neither. The Delaware & Hudson Rail*road* became the Delaware & Hudson Rail*way* under Dereco, while the parent D&H Company, under the new name of Champlain National, took the proceeds of the sale and moved into non-rail fields.

None of this would have happened had Dumaine had his way. From the beginning he was opposed to the N&W takeover, finding the amount the larger road was offering the smaller "grossly inadequate"—or, in less formal terms, "fifty cents on the dollar of a junk value." Beyond that, he believed the D&H should be looking for inclusion in an all-New England system—with the B&M, Maine

Central, and Bangor & Aroostook, and perhaps New Haven—rather than courting the likes of EL and N&W. Nevertheless, the D&H board of directors voted in favor of the Dereco plan.

"I am convinced that the D&H Railroad can continue to operate profitably as an independent carrier," Dumaine declared. To back up his conviction he resigned as president, chief executive officer, and chairman in the early months of 1968 to lead a proxy fight against the board's decision. Dumaine and his associates owned 15.2% of D&H common stock. When the proxy votes were tallied, only 25% favored Dumaine's independent stance for the D&H, while 67% favored merger, with the balance not voting. Thus ended Dumaine's chapter of the D&H story, though he was far from finished with railroading in the northeast. Within a year Dumaine's Amoskeag Company (which owns, among other things, Fieldcrest Mills and Fanny Farmer Candy Shops) bought the Bangor & Aroostook Railroad. Today, Dumaine serves as BAR's chairman and chief executive officer; from that position, he has continued to press hard for an all-New England rail system, beginning with a BAR-Maine Central merger.

After Dumaine's resignation from the D&H, Frank Wells McCabe served as acting president for the few months until the D&H actually came under Dereco control. When it did, John P. Fishwick took over as president. Fishwick was the N&W's senior vice-president and the EL's chairman; thus his assumption of the D&H presidency cemented the Dereco relationship. The D&H had entered a period of management from afar, a period which continued for two years under Fishwick and another two under his successor, Gregory W. Maxwell, who served simultaneously as EL president.

This era of joint D&H-EL management would come to a dramatic close in the early summer of 1972, when the Erie Lackawanna, battered by hurricane Agnes, declared bankruptcy. And even during the intervening years it was business much as usual on both EL and D&H, in spite of Dereco. EL sold D&H four ex-*Phoebe Snow* coaches in September 1970 for use on *The Laurentian* and the *Montreal Limited* and leased some E8's for those trains the following winter. Among the few other readily visible innovations of the joint management were motive-power run-throughs. One example of this, initiated in early 1968, even before D&H officially joined Dereco, was an EL-D&H-B&M power pool on the Boston-Chicago piggybackers PB-99 and PB-100. Though there were other such instances

This page: In October 1968, RS3 No. 4107 drops down into Port Henry on Lake Champlain & Moriah trackage with a trainload of sintered ore from Republic Steel's Mill No. 7. Full retainers have helped ease the train down a 3.96 percent grade. Facing page: Snow-covered Lake Champlain forms a background at Fort Ticonderoga for the RS3-powered local freight working out of Whitehall. ROGER COOK

Facing page, left: Near Thompson, Pa., U33C No. 755 leads a southbound assault of Ararat. Facing page, top right: A westbound freight is seen from the cab of PA No. 18, heading a June 1974 Binghamton-Saratoga Springs excursion. KARL R. ZIMMERMANN

Above: U-boats work south at Thompson. KARL R. ZIMMERMANN

Facing page, bottom right: Under the sand tower at Rouses Point, U30C No. 712 waits out a cold January night in 1976. TOM KELCEC

—among them Mechanicville-Binghamton-Meadville, O., TC-99 and TC-100—they changed the face of the D&H but little.

Much more important was something beneath the surface: the unease almost inescapable for an enterprise not in control of its own destiny. Though D&H entered Dereco in a considerably stronger position than did EL, it was less than one-quarter the latter road's size. D&H men couldn't help feeling that their own railroad's concerns were not likely to receive top priority consideration, when decisions were made in Cleveland or Roanoke, by EL or N&W executives, not in Albany, by D&H people. Though little was done to destroy D&H identity during these years of management by remote control, nothing was done to foster it either.

Things changed radically in this respect after June 1972 when the EL filed for reorganization under Section 77 of the Federal Bankruptcy Act and thus ended its affiliation with Dereco. Maxwell, in order to maintain his position as president and chief executive officer of the EL, had to resign from the D&H. Thus the road's management moved back to Albany and was put in the hands of Carl B. Sterzing, Jr., who had been D&H general counsel for the previous two years, after spending the eight years before that in N&W's legal department. When Sterzing took over the reins of the D&H, the railroad was faltering, and there were many hazards ahead. After years of profitability the road had posted a small loss in 1971 and would go over a million dollars into the red in 1972. But rather

than holding back and being too cautious, Sterzing chose to drive forward vigorously, though with carefully calculated direction. The changes he implemented, taken together, he called the "Program for Survival."

Sterzing began by underlining the D&H's smallness, independence, and consequent ability to render personal service, promoting these virtues to shippers—in contrast to the impersonal hugeness of Penn Central, the D&H's primary competitor. A similar stress on the personal approach became the keynote of the company's internal affairs as well. Sterzing went out among the D&H employees and came to know as many as possible. He reinstituted a monthly newsletter and an annual system-wide inspection trip by rail for management.

Though a proponent of good public, community, and employee relations, Bruce Sterzing was tough—as a derelict employee or unwary competitor could attest. To keep the D&H in business amid failing connections, consolidations treacherous to its future, and continuing preferential treatment of highway and waterway interests, Sterzing had to be strong and able to fight without pulling punches. He had no sooner taken over the D&H than he was given an excellent chance to demonstrate this toughness in an ongoing battle with Penn Central over Buttonwood Yard.

Buttonwood Yard, on the outskirts of Wilkes-Barre, had traditionally been a major Pennsylvania Railroad gateway to the Northeast, via D&H (which reached it from its own Hudson Yard by the seven-mile Wilkes-Barre Connecting Railroad, jointly owned by PRR and D&H). After the Penn Central merger, however, the West Shore-Boston & Albany route took away much of the business. Nevertheless, in 1972, D&H was still receiving 4500 cars a month from the PC at Buttonwood, accounting for approximately $100,000 in revenues. Most were bound for the B&M at Mechanicville.

Top: Under Dereco, EL leased some E8's to D&H. Making their initial run, Nos. 822 and 815 are just beyond Westport with a weather-delayed Montreal Limited *on January 2, 1970.* ROGER COOK

Bottom: Dereco brought power pooling too, as seen on an eastbound approaching Tunnel, N.Y., in April 1972. Facing page, bottom: Six-axle U-boats and Centuries work northbound out of Wilkes-Barre on the Penn Division in January 1972. TOM KELCEC

Facing page, top: RW-6, the "Paper Train," hustles around the big curve at Fort Ann, N.Y. KARL R. ZIMMERMANN

In the board room of D&H's Albany offices, Bruce Sterzing sits before a painting of the Stourbridge Lion. KARL R. ZIMMERMANN

In June 1972, hurricane Agnes, whose devastation of the EL had such important ramifications for the D&H, also washed out portions of the PC's Wilkes-Barre Branch along the Susquehanna River from Buttonwood to Sunbury, Pa. The PC sought to abandon the line entirely and instead deliver D&H traffic at Schenectady, N. Y. This change, PC argued, would cut delivery time by two or three days, save $1.5 million annually in operating costs, and still give the D&H approximately the same revenue split.

Sterzing didn't buy this proposal, which would have cut the D&H haul from 216 to 16 miles; he reasoned that shippers would soon not bother to specify a mere 16 miles of D&H and would slide to an all-PC routing. Thus D&H offered very publicly to give PC $100,000 to rebuild its Sunbury line or to do the job gratis with D&H maintenance-of-way forces. Then D&H petitioned the ICC to force PC to reopen the line. Meanwhile, beginning September 18, 1972, traffic was being detoured over the Erie Lackawanna's Bloomsburg Branch, from the D&H connection at Plymouth Junction (across the Susquehanna River from Buttonwood) to the PC at Northumberland. D&H won its point, but it was not until August 25, 1973, that the Wilkes-Barre Branch was finally reopened.

By that time, another piece of trackage—this a new section, and very short though very important—was in place, also in the Wilkes-Barre area: the connection with the Lehigh Valley at Dupont. Opened on February 3, 1973, it made possible the vigorous promotion of a pair of run-through freights: NE-84 and NE-87, which operated between Rigby Yard in Portland, Me., and Potomac Yard in Alexandria, Va., traveling via B&M-D&H-LV-Reading-Baltimore & Ohio. D&H and LV pooled power, as did B&O and RDG. The NE-84/NE-87 pair had been started in 1970, with the Jersey Central as the middle link, turning over traffic to D&H at the yard in downtown Wilkes-Barre. When CNJ terminated operations in Pennsylvania on March 31, 1972, LV stepped in to complete the chain, though the inconvenient, time-consuming interchange at Wilkes-Barre remained. It took the Dupont connection to make this "Northeast Alphabet Route"—so called because of the large number of railroads involved—a serious competitor to Penn Central's Northeast Corridor and West Shore routes.

Though just one of five participating carriers, the D&H was particularly aggressive in promoting the NE-84/NE-87 service. The most dramatic device used to this end was an inspection trip—jointly sponsored by B&M and D&H, but using D&H equipment exclusively—from Rigby to "Pot Yard" on March 19-21, 1974. This seven-car special, led by PA's Nos. 17 and 18, with business cars No. 500 and 200 bringing up the rear, carried representatives from the U. S. Department of Transportation, Federal Railway Administration, and ICC, as well as state government officials and members of the press. The message to those aboard, many of whom could be expected to have a hand in shaping the Northeast's rail future, was that PC didn't have all the good routes.

This Northeast Alphabet special followed in what had already become a small tradition of inspection trains, begun not long after Sterzing's installation as D&H president in July 1972. Sterzing's first annual system-wide directors' special ran on November 29 and 30. In the consist were one of the four coaches which had been purchased from the EL in 1970 for *Laurentian* service; ex-D&RGW buffet lounge *Castle Gate,* renamed *Champlain* for the occasion; EL 10 roomette-5 double-bedroom sleeper *Spirit of Youngstown* (which a few years later would wear Conrail blue as one of its official cars); and office cars Nos. 200 and 500. The power was resurrected PA's Nos. 18 and 19.

A trio of Lehigh Valley "Snowbird" Century 628's crosses the trestle at Starrucca, Pa., in their climb to the summit of Ararat. It's May 27, 1973, and today the pushers are a U-boat and an RS36. KARL R. ZIMMERMANN

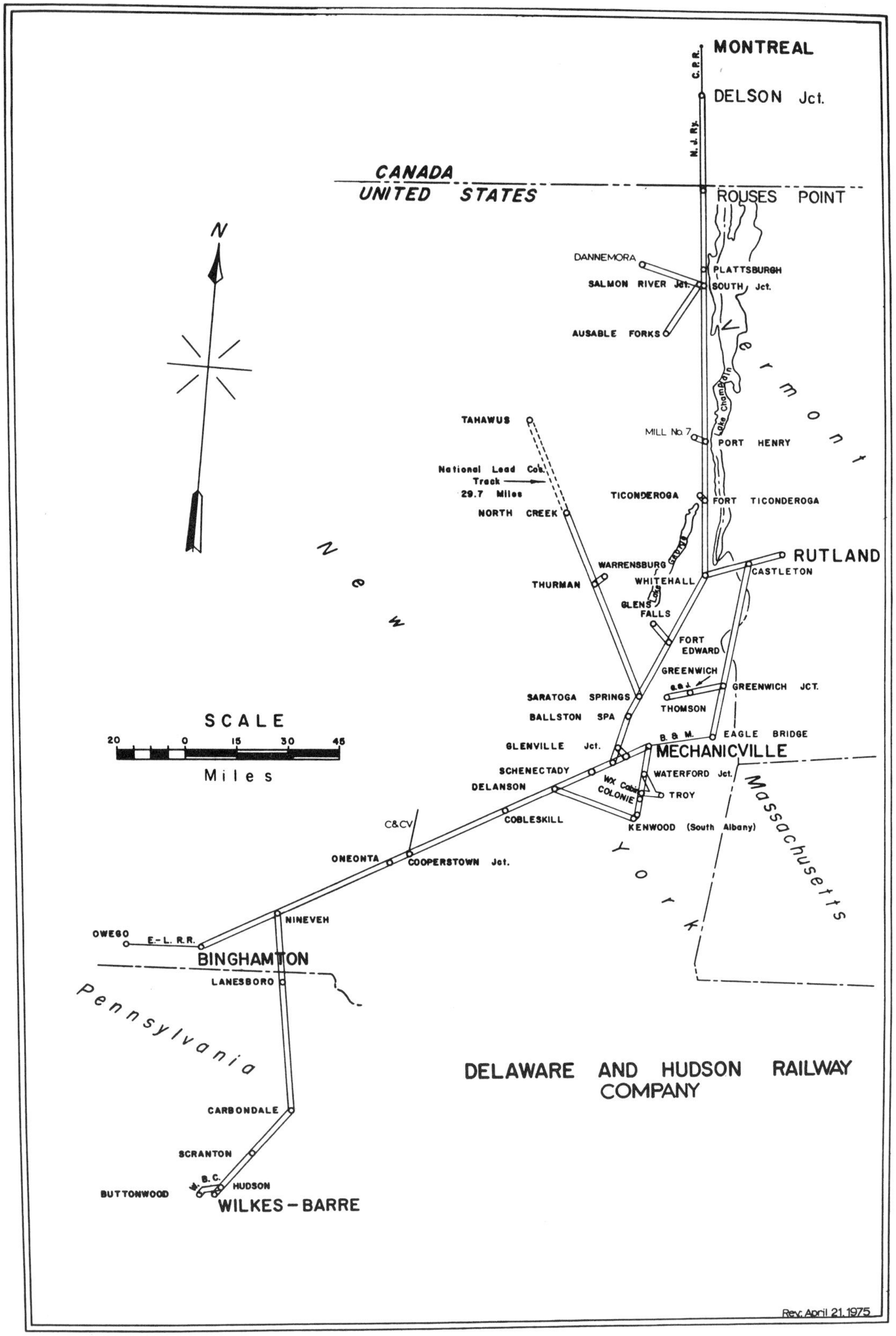

MONTREAL
C.R.R.
DELSON Jct.
N.J. Ry.
CANADA
UNITED STATES
ROUSES POINT
N
DANNEMORA
PLATTSBURGH
SALMON RIVER Jct.
SOUTH Jct.
AUSABLE FORKS
Vermont
Lake Champlain
TAHAWUS
MILL No. 7
PORT HENRY
National Lead Co. Track 29.7 Miles
TICONDEROGA
FORT TICONDEROGA
NORTH CREEK
RUTLAND
CASTLETON
WARRENSBURG
Lake George
WHITEHALL
THURMAN
GLENS FALLS
New
FORT EDWARD
GREENWICH
GREENWICH JCT.
SARATOGA SPRINGS
THOMSON
BALLSTON SPA
SCALE
20 0 15 30 45
Miles
B. & M.
EAGLE BRIDGE
GLENVILLE Jct.
MECHANICVILLE
SCHENECTADY
WATERFORD Jct.
DELANSON
WX Cabin
COLONIE
TROY
Massachusetts
C&CV
COBLESKILL
KENWOOD (South Albany)
ONEONTA
COOPERSTOWN Jct.
York
NINEVEH
OWEGO
E.-L. R.R.
BINGHAMTON
LANESBORO
Pennsylvania
DELAWARE AND HUDSON RAILWAY COMPANY
CARBONDALE
SCRANTON
W. B. C.
HUDSON
BUTTONWOOD
WILKES-BARRE
Rev. April 21, 1975

Top: Pooled power—Centuries from the Lehigh Valley—roll west past the yard office in Oneonta, N.Y. GEORGE BERISSO

Bottom: In February 1976, NE-84, the Portland, Me.-Alexandria, Va., run-through, crosses the Lehigh River on the LV at White Haven. KARL R. ZIMMERMANN

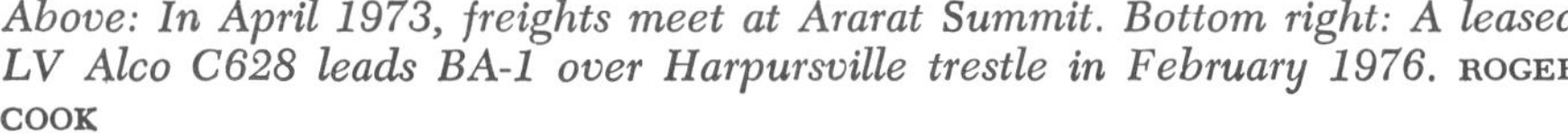

Above: In April 1973, freights meet at Ararat Summit. Bottom right: A leased LV Alco C628 leads BA-1 over Harpursville trestle in February 1976. ROGER COOK

Top right: On the NE-84/NE-87 and CX-1/CX-2 trains, cabooses as well as locomotives were pooled by D&H and LV. Here, D&H pushers shove behind an LV buggy at Lanesboro, Pa., bound for Ararat. KARL R. ZIMMERMANN

17
18

These lanky passenger Alcos were a story in themselves, one spanning the entire 1967-1977 decade. They never had much directly to do with the D&H's bread-and-butter business of moving freight (though they themselves were tonnage haulers for a brief time), but they attracted an enormous amount of attention to the D&H, and not just among railroad fans either. In a curious way, the health of these four diesels mirrored the prosperity of the D&H as a whole during the ten years they were on the property.

When Santa Fe's roughly twenty-year-old Alco PA's Nos. 59, 60, 62, and 66 rolled out of the West to become D&H Nos. 16-19, the PA era for the rest of the country was closing. The Denver & Rio Grande Western and Southern Pacific had shut down their big Alcos, and Erie Lackawanna and Santa Fe would soon do the same. When they did, that left D&H's quartet as the sole survivors of this much admired breed of diesel. (Actually, the D&H also acquired a fifth PA, ex-New Haven No. 0783, purchased from General Electric in February 1968 for parts.)

From their introduction into *Laurentian* and *Montreal Limited* service in the waning days of 1967 until May 1, 1971, when Amtrak took over those trains and scuttled them, the PA's were the most glamorous, most photographed, most discussed diesels in America. After that, however, they quickly became the most surplus, for standardization-minded Amtrak was in the market for Electro-Motive Division E8's and E9's or, in a pinch, that builder's passenger-equipped F's. Clearly, the PA's would never wear Amtrak's red, blue, and platinum mist. They seemed to have little future of any kind.

Before long Nos. 16 and 19 were sent to General Electric's Erie plant as trade-ins against future diesel purchases by D&H. Nos. 17 and 18—thanks in large measure to Bruce Sterzing, D&H general counsel at the time—went to a seemingly more auspicious fate; they were acquired by Steam Tours Inc., of Akron, O., on a six-month lease-with-option-to-purchase. This fan-trip operator managed just two excursions with the PA's before damage to a main bearing on No. 16, coupled with general financial woes, led Steam Tours to return the Alcos to the D&H.

They came back in August 1972, the month after Bruce Sterzing became president. Sterzing was enough of a rail enthusiast and historian to be aware that the PA's were something special. Unquestionably, he was proud that these rare diesels—true "living history"

Facing page: PA's Nos. 18 and 17 power an October 1974 "Penn Division Special" northbound near Windsor, N. Y. KARL R. ZIMMERMANN

Above: On this April 1974 special, a trio of PA's—Nos. 18, 19 and 17—work through Starrucca, Pa., returning from Oneonta to Hudson Yard in Wilkes-Barre. GEORGE KELCEC

exhibits by this time—were on his railroad's roster. Furthermore, nearly alone among railroad executives, he welcomed the interest of the fans, such as the PA's provoked. Therefore, he recalled the remaining pair of PA's, Nos. 17 and 18, from GE; technically, they were still the D&H's, since the road had ordered no new power since they were sent to Erie as trade-ins. Then Sterzing authorized the operation of excursions with these charismatic locomotives. The initial venture was the September 29, 1973, "Susquehanna Valley Special," a Binghamton-Albany round-trip powered by a trio of the Alcos—just the first of many such outings.

Left: On June 29, 1974, as skies threaten thunderstorms, PA's Nos. 18 and 17—pulling a special from Binghamton to the "Spirit of America" fair in Saratoga—leave Cobleskill under a characteristic canopy of PA exhaust. Facing page, left: In October 1974, these same two PA's deadhead a consist north near Forest City, Pa., following a Penn Division excursion. These views clearly illustrate the EMD-style grille applied to No. 17 while the locomotive was owned by Santa Fe. Like the locomotive's "warbonnet" paint scheme, the grille lingered through the D&H years—despite efforts to find an original Alco grille as a cosmetic replacement. KARL R. ZIMMERMANN

Facing page, right: Cresting Richmondville Hill on the May 26, 1974, excursion from Albany to Starrucca Viaduct in Lanesboro, Pa. ROGER COOK

Though these excursions delighted the fans—which in turn delighted Sterzing and the D&H—management was casting a wider net than this in operating them. For one thing, the PA's and the passenger excursions were intended as a focal point for company pride among employees. For another, the local populace enjoyed the chance simply to take a train ride, for sight-seeing or just the nostalgia of it. The autumn "Leaf-Peaker Specials" up the superbly scenic Adirondack Branch to North Creek, N. Y., were among the most popular trips. The PA's were certainly not performing for rail buffs only. They played to a wider audience: regional shippers and others whose good will might eventually benefit the D&H. Surveys have repeatedly shown that, however overwhelmingly preeminent is freight service in the rail system's hierarchy of priorities, the general public still associates trains with passenger service. To many, no passenger train equals no railroad. Thus, Sterzing reasoned, shiny PA's and snappy blue, gray, and yellow coaches could certainly do the D&H's public image no harm, and quite likely could do some good.

To this same end was one of the repossessed PA's first assignments, months before the initial excursion. In 1973 the D&H would

Top left: Nos. 18, 19, and 17 on the May 1974 excursion to Starrucca Viaduct. ROBERT MOHOWSKI

Bottom: Eastbound on that same excursion, descending Richmondville Hill. ROGER COOK

Top right: Southbound at Scranton, on the previous month's "Penn Division Special." TOM KELCEC

celebrate its sesquicentennial, an occasion rich in possibilities for its grass-roots public-relations campaign. Thus the railroad did a number of splashy things to mark its 150th. It commissioned a handsome painting by Manville Wakefield, which spanned the century and a half by juxtaposing canal boats with a contemporary freight train hauled by GE "U-boats." D&H held a V.I.P. luncheon on April 23, the sesquicentennial day, and an employees' ball on May 19, with 900 guests in attendance. In addition, it put together a display train to tour the system, and this was how PA's Nos. 18 and 19 got into the act.

This road show had buffet lounge *Champlain,* for entertaining guests, coupled in behind the locomotives. Next was a flat car bearing a replica of the *Stourbridge Lion,* built at Colonie Shops in 1933 for the Century of Progress Exposition in Chicago. (The original *Lion,* with railroad pioneer Horatio Allen at the throttle, had on August 8, 1829, been the first steam locomotive to operate in the United States when it rolled over D&H Canal Company trackage.) There were two baggage cars with D&H memorabilia and models, a boxcar, and a caboose. Between April 23 and May 12, the train visited sixteen communities along the railroad, reinforcing a positive image of the D&H for the thousands who ogled the PA's and toured the exhibits.

The D&H handed out one additional favor at its sesquicentennial party. On April 28 and 29, the line ran a steam excursion from Albany to Montreal and return, with double-heading on certain segments of the trip. More remarkable still, the two locomotives involved had been touched up at Colonie Shops to suggest ghosts from D&H's past.

The original plan had been to run with just Steamtown's ex-Canadian Pacific G5 4-6-2 No. 127. However, heavy demand for tickets led the D&H to look for a more powerful locomotive; the railroad found ex-Reading T1 Northern No. 2102, owned by Steam Tours (one-time lessee of the PA's) but operating under High Iron Company aegis. The next step in the trip's evolution was the decision to use both engines. The Pacific was given a pair of the "elephant-ear" smoke deflectors that had distinguished D&H steam locomotives and the D&H P1 number 653—but still looked very CPR. The Reading T1's transformation to D&H K class No. 302 was more successful and included—in addition to smoke deflectors—vee numberboards, protruding "bug-eye" marker lights, and a recessed headlight.

The sesquicentennial display train—with PA's Nos. 18 and 19, buffet lounge Champlain, *the* Stourbridge Lion *on a flat car, a box car, two baggage cars, and a caboose is about to duck under Starrucca Viaduct.*
KARL R. ZIMMERMANN

Top right: The sesquicentennial logo. ROGER COOK

Top center: Manville Wakefield's sesquicentennial painting, as it later appeared on the Adirondack service plate. On the northbound leg of the steam excursion, counterfeit P1 No. 653 waits in the rain at Port Henry (right). Shortly thereafter, Nos. 653 and 302 leave town doubleheaded (above). KARL R. ZIMMERMANN

Top: At dusk, the locomotives drift into Coopersville for a photo runby. Bottom: The next day, on the return leg of the excursion, just Northern No. 302 is in charge at Port Kent. The office car is No. 200.
KARL R. ZIMMERMANN

These facsimile locomotives were not meant to fool anybody, of course, but rather to help the observer recall the long and hearty history of the D&H. This they did. The trip was a huge success in spite of dreary weather. Twenty-two carloads of happy excursionists listened as the Pacific's blood-tingling chime whistle played counterpoint to the Northern's deep-throated steamboat sounds; they watched misty Lake Champlain slide by; they looked on as double-shotted steam roared through a photo runby, with President Sterzing at the throttle of the Pacific.

Though the various sesquicentennial festivities together were a highlight of 1973, much more important in the long run was the fact that the loss for that year was cut to just $198,000, down from over a million dollars the previous year. Also in 1973, D&H learned that it had won the Edward H. Harriman Memorial Gold Medal for employee safety for 1972, the first of four consecutive years the railroad would receive this honor. Sterzing's "Program for Survival" was proceeding strongly, and the D&H was more than surviving. It was almost prospering.

An even better year was 1974, which brought a million dollar profit, the second Gold Medal for safety, and a public relations splash more showy than the sesquicentennial doings. This gambit—which eventually turned out to be other than an absolute blessing—was the D&H's participation in *The Adirondack*, a second Amtrak passenger train on the New York-Montreal route.

The D&H's Champlain Subdivision is about as gloriously scenic a line for a passenger train as any in the country. For much of the 112 miles from Rouses Point to Whitehall, the tracks run hard by the shore of Lake Champlain—sometimes near water level, other times high above, as when the rails thread the spectacular Red Rocks at Willsboro Bay. For this natural splendor as much as for the blue-and-yellow PA's, the discontinuance at Amtrak's inception of both *The Laurentian* and the *Montreal Limited* had been much lamented.

Top: The northbound excursion at Port Kent. Bottom: At Fort Edward, children scurry to trackside in the train's wake, looking for flattened coins. KARL R. ZIMMERMANN

Facing page: The Belden Hill pushers run light across Harpursville trestle on a sunny February day. ROGER COOK

617
DELAWARE & HUDSON
604

Top: Southbound at Carbondale, Pa., in April 1974. Facing page, top: Three years earlier, an eastbound out of Binghamton is about to enter the bore at Tunnel, N.Y. TOM KELCEC

Bottom: At the south end of the yard at Whitehall, a local freight from Saratoga Springs arrives behind an RS11 and an RS3, meeting a Century-powered RW-6 waiting to depart. KARL R. ZIMMERMANN

Facing page, bottom: A westbound blasts through Tunnel. The pair of U-boats on the point are helpers. ROGER COOK

Amtrak's decision, in 1972, to add a New York-Montreal train to its basic system just added insult to injury for the upstate New Yorkers who had lost their D&H service, since the government passenger corporation chose to place its overnight *Montrealer/Washingtonian* on the longer, slower route via PC, B&M, and CV, through Connecticut, Massachusetts, and Vermont. In spite of their extensive lobbying for the placement of these trains on the D&H route, New York State interests had been spurned. Later, when enthusiasm for the passenger train was temporarily rekindled by the energy crisis of the mid-1970's, state officials decided to take matters into their own hands.

The voters did their part by passing the $30-million Rail Service Preservation Program promoted by Malcolm Wilson, then the governor of New York. Wilson then sought some highly visible demonstration of activity under the program—something like a daylight passenger service on the PC-D&H New York City-Montreal route. Such a service could be initiated under the 403b provision of the Amtrak law, which allowed a state to sponsor additional Amtrak trains by paying two-thirds of their operating losses. Unlike many railroads faced with similar requests, the D&H was happy to run a train for the New York Department of Transportation and Amtrak—but on its own terms.

In order to reap the greatest possible public relations benefit, Sterzing insisted that the train be operated with D&H cars, locomotives, and crews—all clearly wearing D&H logos, letterboards, and pins or patches. Temporarily short of coaches, Amtrak agreed to these terms, as did the New York DOT, so wheels were set in motion that would lead to the train's August 5, 1974, inauguration as *The Adirondack*—renamed for New York State's mountains instead of Quebec's Laurentians. New York State—which in addition to paying two-thirds of the train's operating losses had committed $3.2 million for track rehabilitation, station renovation and construction, and locomotive and passenger car rebuilding—felt entitled to make this chauvinistic change.

The most remarkable aspect of the *Adirondack* project was perhaps this: The locomotives to be rebuilt were the PA's, which had begun to seem positively feline in multiplicity of lives. Nos. 16 and 19 were sent to Morrison-Knudsen Company in Boise, Ida., in late June of 1974; Nos. 17 and 18 stayed behind awhile to power *The Adirondack* on its inaugural and afterward. Later, they in turn

headed west to M-K, upon the return first of No. 19 (on March 1, 1975) and then of No. 16. Each unit left the D&H as a 2000-horsepower PA1 and returned as a PA4, carrying in its belly a new 2400-horsepower engine built at Auburn, N. Y., by the Alco Engines Division of the White Motor Corporation.

After their return, two of the locomotives were given names. No. 16 had "M. A. Davis" inscribed beneath the cab window on the engineer's side, honoring the line's General Road Foreman of Engines. Davis, whose retirement in the summer of 1977 was to break yet another tie with the past, had become known to some as "Mr. PA." A man of unusual warmth and personal magnetism, he took true delight and pride in the Alcos; he liked to run them, particularly on excursions, when there would be plenty of children at trackside for him to wave to and salute with the PA's melodic chime horns. The other named locomotive, No. 18, honored George W. Hockaday, the D&H's Senior Mechanical Engineer, whose skillful ministrations at Colonie Shop had kept the PA's on the road through the decade.

Hoover Industries, in Miami, Fla., was selected to rebuild the *Adirondack* passenger cars, all of them veterans of *Laurentian* service. Sent to Florida immediately for refurbishing were ex-D&RGW baggage-mail cars Nos. 51 and 52 and diner-lounges Nos. 41 and 42, *Mt. Timpanogos* and *James Peak,* to be renamed *Saratoga Inn* and *Adirondack Lodge.* The five coaches which had arrived with these cars in 1967 had been sold in 1972 to Colombia's Ferrocarriles Nacionales, so D&H dug deeper into its boneyard. It found four from among the six Raymond Loewy-styled coaches delivered to the D&H by American Car and Foundry in the fall of 1939, for an earlier version of *The Laurentian.* The four ex-EL *Phoebe Snow* coaches were held back to provide interim service on *The Adirondack;* all four originally were slated to go in turn to Hoover for refurbishing as the ACF cars came back completed, but only two were ever actually sent.

The problem of what stand-in cars to operate while the others

Left: the southbound Adirondack *nears Whitehall.* ROGER COOK

Facing page: At Rouses Point, the kerosine markers habitually used on the train while running in Canada have been removed from the leased CP Rail "Skyline" dome car and replaced with electric flashers. The Adirondack's *drumhead provided a touch of class virtually unknown elsewhere in the United States in 1974, the year the photograph was taken.* KARL R. ZIMMERMANN

THE ADIRONDACK

were being refurbished was a thorny one, and one which proved to have serious consequences for the long-term health of the train. Two ex-Erie heavyweights—Nos. 1001 and 1012, purchased from the EL—were pressed into service; though pleasant, comfortable cars in spite of their age, they fell far short of the goal of luxurious modernity intended for the train. Even less satisfactory was elderly coach No. 229—named *C. J. Brierley* for *The Adirondack*'s senior conductor—an ex-D&H, ex-Boston & Albany heavyweight leased from the Central New York Chapter of the National Railway Historical Society. Most unsatisfactory of all were a group of rag-tag commuter coaches leased from New York's Metropolitan Transportation Authority.

The one very positive feature of *The Adirondack*'s interim equipping was the pair of "Skyline" domes leased from the Canadian Pacific. Temporarily named *Willsboro Point* and *Bluff Point*, with "Delaware and Hudson" spelled out in blue on a yellow letterboard, these buffet lounge-dome coaches of *Canadian* and *Dominion* ancestry were used by the D&H to provide food service, which they did surprisingly well considering how small the dining area was. *Willsboro Point* and *Bluff Point* introduced domes to a route that richly deserved them.

The Adirondack's inaugural run, for press and dignitaries, took place on August 5, 1974, with all the requisite hoopla. The four *Phoebe Snow* coaches ran up from New York City to Albany-Rensselaer, where they were added to a consist of ex-Erie heavyweights Nos. 1001 and 1012, buffet lounge-dome *Willsboro Point*, buffet lounge *Champlain*, and office car 200. On the point were PA's Nos. 17 and 18. The entire nine-car train, plus the pair of diesels, gleamed in Champlain blue and yellow, set off by silver, stainless steel, or gray. It was, as Sterzing had planned, a rolling advertisement for the D&H. Bands played, crowds gathered, and politicians—Governor Malcolm Wilson in particular—orated, all *de rigeur* for an inaurgural. It was a great occasion, filled with excitement and high hopes for *The Adirondack*.

In March 1975, Adirondack *power was either a PA not yet sent to Morrison-Knudsen—as in this scene at Fort Ticonderoga (top)—or Nos. 1508 and 1536, a pair of steam-generator-equipped RS3's leased from B&M, shown at Whitehall (bottom). Facing page:* The Adirondack *is RS-powered through the Red Rocks.* KARL R. ZIMMERMANN

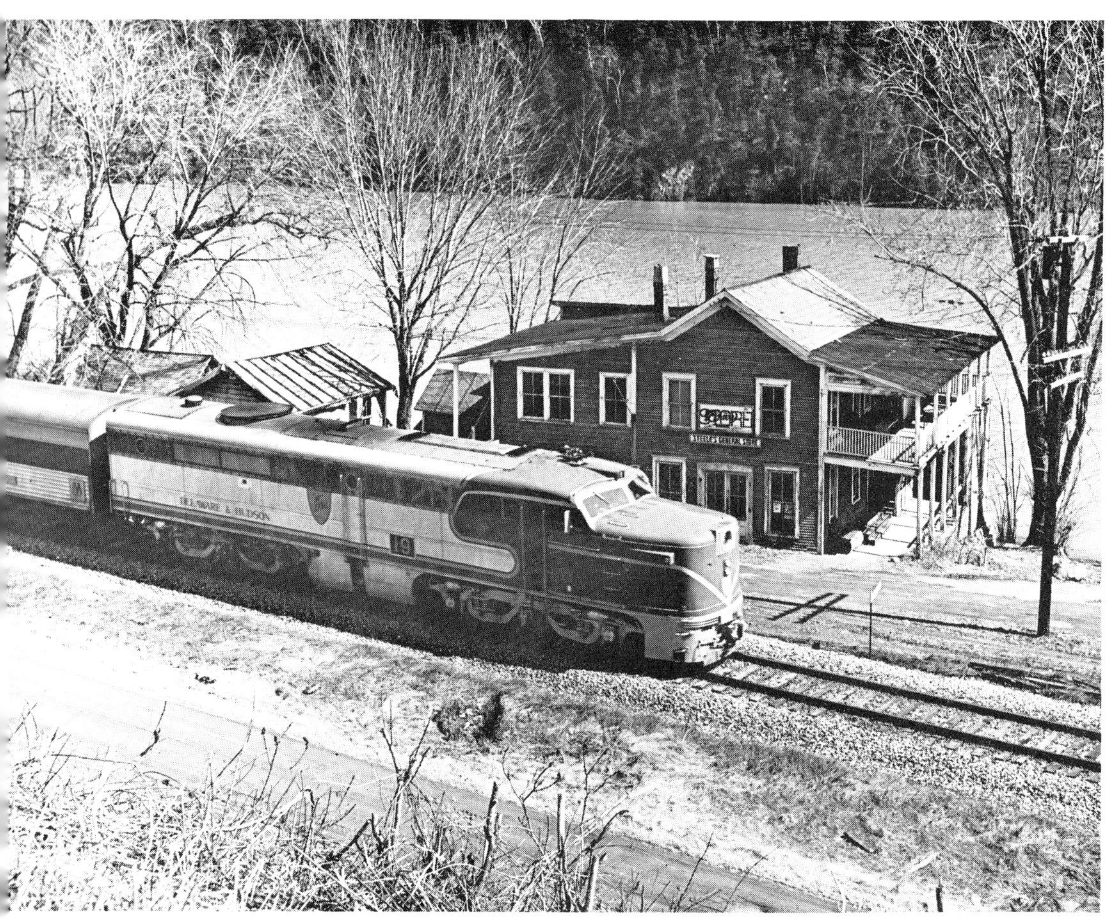

Top: PA's roll southbound past the general store at Dresden Station (left) and northbound out of Whitehall (right). KARL R. ZIMMERMANN

Bottom: Returning from the Quebec Winter Carnival in February 1975, privately owned ex-PRR business car Pennsylvania *and heavyweight Pullman* Clover Colony *bring up the rear of* The Adirondack *at Fort Ticonderoga.* ROGER COOK

The following day, a little reality entered the scene, in the form of the train's first northbound revenue run. The consist, behind a glamorless pair of Alcos, RS11 No. 5004 and RS36 No. 5020, was three MTA coaches and CP dome *Bluff Point.* The presence of these MTA coaches was to do great harm to *The Adirondack* in the months ahead, as they were simply not acceptable for long-distance travel. When the *Phoebe Snow* coaches were sidelined with mechanical problems, as frequently happened, and particularly after Nos. 31 and 33 had been sent to Florida, only the MTA cars were available. (The heavyweights had to stay north of Albany; because of their friction-bearing trucks, Amtrak would not operate them.) If one of the domes was out of service, buffet lounge *Champlain,* which had been handsomely refurbished for company use at Colonie Shops, generally filled in.

The equipment problem was made particularly acute and frustrating by delays at Hoover Industries. Not until the early spring of 1975 did completed cars begin to arrive back on the D&H. The first to appear were baggage-mails Nos. 51 and 52 and diner-lounges Nos. 41 and 42, *Saratoga Inn* and *Adirondack Lodge.* The baggage cars were used only briefly, but the diner-lounges were very important to the train and in fact became its keynote cars. For passengers, there was just one negative implication of their arrival: It allowed the D&H to return the CP domes, for which it had been paying an exorbitant daily rental. (After a six-month hiatus, Amtrak would provide a pair of dome coaches as replacements.)

Saratoga Inn and *Adirondack Lodge* were the showpieces of the refurbished train. At one end of each car was a lounge area, with comfortable if somewhat oversized chairs. The dining room was at the other end, and the kitchen in the middle. In both dining room and lounge, raised white letters on brown-carpeted bulkheads proclaimed the car's name to passengers. Glass, not the lexan favored by Amtrak, was used for the windows throughout these cars and the refurbished coaches yet to be completed. The walls of each of the diner-lounges, and this would also be the case with the coaches, were hung with historic photographs relating to the name of that particular car. Aboard *Saratoga Inn,* for instance, were views of that on-line city's famous, now-vanished hotels—the Clarendon, the Grand Union, the United States—plus its handsome Victorian residences and its horse racing. (Among the coaches, some projected car names—Crown Point, Valcour Island—were rejected because no suitable illustration was available.) Taped music played in the diner-lounge; this feature was to have been extended throughout the train as soon as refurbished (and thus audio-equipped) cars were used exclusively, but that day never came.

In the dining area, six tables were laid with blue and yellow napery. A small lamp stood on each table. Special china had been created for the train, featuring a scalloped, blue-lined border, the traditional D&H script logo, and a multi-colored New York State coat of arms. (Conspicuously missing from the china and everything else was the Amtrak logo.) Beverages were served in stemmed glassware. The menu cover carried a picture of a PA-powered *Laurentian* in the Red Rocks; the dishes listed inside were conventional, but had names taken from the local area: Champlain Valley Farm Breakfast, Fort Ticonderoga Special, and so on.

The exteriors of *Saratoga Inn* and *Adirondack Lodge* were painted D&H blue, gray, and yellow. From these and the baggage-mail cars, the cosmetic stainless-steel fluting that Pullman-Standard applied below the windows had been removed, so the cars were a perfect match for the already smooth-sided ACF and *Phoebe Snow* coaches when these began to arrive back on the property. First to come was No. 204, *Lake George,* an ACF car. The renovation required on these 35-year-old veterans was extensive and included new aircraft-style seating. Close on No. 204's heels, therefore, was ex-EL No. 31, *Ausable River,* though it and No. 33 had gone to Florida considerably later than the ACF's.

But it was already a year after the inaugural and only a few of the refurbished cars had been completed. Furthermore, those that had been put in service seemed frequently to develop problems, and thus spent far too much time awaiting repair at Colonie. Partly as a result of these equipment deficiencies, *The Adirondack* never did grow strong. The expected ridership never developed; in fact, patronage dwindled to near nothing on some weekdays in winter.

A second plague affecting the health of *The Adirondack* was the ongoing feud that developed between Amtrak and the D&H. Its origin apparently lay in Amtrak's resentment of D&H's jealous guardianship of the train's identity and zealous promotion of its own role in the operation. Since all other railroads which had contracted with Amtrak to run trains were more than happy to keep their names and logos out of sight, the passenger corporation

Top: The Adirondack *at Port Henry (left) and at Rouses Point, with office car No. 500 carrying the markers in February 1976, just before Turboliners took over (right).* KARL R. ZIMMERMANN

Bottom: PA No. 17, Adirondack Lodge, *and three coaches northbound at Port Kent in April 1975.* ROGER COOK

seemed unsure how to respond when D&H had just the opposite wish. Once challenged, Amtrak became as protective of its "pointless arrow" logo as D&H was of its traditional script. This clash was most dramatically highlighted on the occasion when the Amtrak dome coaches first entered *Adirondack* service. Immediately painters at Colonie covered over Amtrak's red and blue on the cars' window bands with D&H yellow and blue. Amtrak protested strenuously, and its colors reappeared posthaste.

Unfortunately, there were disagreements on matters of more substance than paint, and many of them centered on the diner-lounges, particularly whether or not they would operate on the non-D&H portion of the run—from Albany to New York City. (Since clearances at Grand Central Terminal prohibited running the leased CP domes in, this question had not arisen while they were providing

Diner-lounges Saratoga Inn *and* Adirondack Lodge *were the first refurbished cars to be placed in service. Here, at Albany-Rensselaer on April 20, 1975, a car knocker walks past* Saratoga Inn *while passengers detrain from ex-*Phoebe Snow *coach No. 34—then named* Whiteface Mountain*—which never did find its way to Hoover Industries for refurbishing.* KARL R. ZIMMERMANN

ROSTER OF LIGHTWEIGHT PASSENGER CARS

Number	Type	Date Acquired or Built	Names/Comments
21	52-seat coach	10/67 from D&RGW	sold 8/72 to Colombia's Ferrocarriles Nacionales
22	52-seat coach	10/67 from D&RGW	sold 8/72 to Colombia's Ferrocarriles Nacionales
23	52-seat coach	10/67 from D&RGW	sold 8/72 to Colombia's Ferrocarriles Nacionales
24	52-seat coach	10/67 from D&RGW	sold 8/72 to Colombia's Ferrocarriles Nacionales
25	52-seat coach	10/67 from D&RGW	sold 8/72 to Colombia's Ferrocarriles Nacionales
31*	62-seat coach	9/70 from EL	Ausable River
32	62-seat coach	9/70 from EL	temporarily named Bulwagga Bay
33*	62-seat coach	9/70 from EL	Schroon Lake (temporarily Mt. Marcy)
34	62-seat coach	9/70 from EL	temporarily named Whiteface Mountain
35	buffet lounge-dome-coach	leased from CP	Willsboro Point
36	buffet lounge-dome-coach	leased from CP	Bluff Point
41*	diner-lounge	10/67 from D&RGW	Saratoga Inn (originally Mt. Timpanogos)
42*	diner-lounge	10/67 from D&RGW	Adirondack Lodge (originally James Peak)
43	buffet lounge	10/67 from D&RGW	Champlain (originally Castle Gate)
51*	baggage-mail	10/67 from D&RGW	
52*	baggage-mail	10/67 from D&RGW	
53	baggage-mail	10/67 from D&RGW	
56	baggage	10/67 from D&RGW	Town of Stillwater (sold 1977 to Chessie)
201	76-seat coach	9-10/39 from ACF	
202*	76-seat coach	9-10/39 from ACF	Lake Placid
203	76-seat coach	9-10/39 from ACF	
204*	76-seat coach	9-10/39 from ACF	Lake George
205*	76-seat coach	9-10/39 from ACF	Fort Ticonderoga
206*	76-seat coach	9-10/39 from ACF	Essex County

* Refurbished at Hoover Industries, Miami, Fla., for Adirondack service.

the food service.) D&H was more than a little proud of its spanking-new diner-lounges and was hesitant to subject them to the slap-dash cleaning, stocking, and maintenance that could be expected at Grand Central. D&H fears proved justified; the cars returned from GCT filthy and ill-provisioned, and the only way to get them into Colonie for proper cleaning was to run a round-trip without a diner or to cycle in the *Champlain*. But the D&H had other uses for the *Champlain* and thus was not anxious to contribute it regularly.

On the other hand, Amtrak remained adamant in its insistence that dining service on the Albany-Grand Central portion of the run was essential to the train's success. The conflict on this issue resulted in D&H's unilaterally pulling back the diner-lounges to its own rails; Amtrak's unilaterally pulling off its dining-car crews, leaving the D&H to recruit cooks and waitresses virtually overnight; and an eventual uneasy compromise which had the diners running through to GCT, with D&H crews working north of Albany and Amtrak crews south.

After demonstrating its alienation from the yellow, blue, and gray D&H *Adirondack* by providing for it only the skimpiest advertising and no incentive fares, Amtrak on March 1, 1977, played its trump card: It introduced Rohr-built Turboliner trainsets on the route, the only graceful way it could force the retirement of D&H's conventional equipment. At the same time, Amtrak reduced fares and increased advertising. Coupled with the lure of new equipment, these innovations brought substantial ridership increases to *The Adirondack*—though some observers deeply regretted the loss of the domes and diner-lounges, feeling the route to be both too long and too scenic to justify their omission.

Facing page: The Amtrak dome coach in this southbound Adirondack *must be well patronized during its passage through the Red Rocks.* TOM KELCEC

Left: At Windsor Station in Montreal, the Amtrak logo is conspicuously absent. Above: After refurbishing, ACF coach No. 204 is Lake George. KARL R. ZIMMERMANN

But by this time the D&H and President Sterzing had other, more pressing problems to deal with, and they involved a government agency other than Amtrak. As mandated by the Regional Rail Reorganization Act of 1973, the United States Railway Association was attempting to put the pieces back together again for Northeastern railroading, left in chaos by the bankruptcies of the Penn Central, Erie Lackawanna, Reading, Lehigh Valley, Jersey Central, and others. The reconstruction would take shape as Conrail, freight-hauling cousin to Amtrak, and the glue would be some $2.03 billion in Federal funds.

Through 1975 the D&H watched developments uneasily, fully aware that it stood to lose its friendly connections to the south and west. In fact, with the exception of the Canadian National, Canadian Pacific, Central Vermont, and Boston & Maine, all of the D&H's Class I connections were to be included in Conrail. Once again, the D&H would be extremely vulnerable because of its innate and unalterable personality: It was a bridge route, dependent for traffic on its connections at both ends.

Maintenance of competition was one of the clearly stated goals of the Rail Act of 1973—the 'Three R" or Conrail Act—and USRA was expected to promote this end. Agreement came early that the D&H would extend its reach in two directions: south to Allentown, Pa., via trackage rights over Conrail's ex-Lehigh Valley route; and west to Enola Yard at Harrisburg, Pa., via purchase of PC's Wilkes-Barre Branch and trackage rights over ex-PC Conrail from Sunbury to Enola. But more important, it was USRA's best hope that Chessie System would acquire substantial portions of Reading and Erie Lackawanna, thus becoming a true competitor to Conrail—and a friendly connection to D&H.

Though Chessie was in principle agreeable to this northeasterly expansion, the plan fell through when the railroad and the union brotherhoods failed to reach an agreement by February 11, 1976, the deadline. This failure initiated a period of frantic activity in the D&H Albany offices. In a miracle of expedition, the following

Facing page: North of Port Henry in the summer of 1976. TOM KELCEC

Top: At Albany-Rensselaer, Amtrak E8's take over from D&H PA's to forward The Adirondack *to New York City.* KARL R. ZIMMERMANN

Bottom: Turboliner at Whitehall in its first month. ROGER COOK

additional extensions of D&H operations were arranged by March 5, when a chartered plane flew the pertinent agreement south to USRA in Washington: D&H trains would run to Oak Island Yard in Newark, N. J., via ex-LV; to Park Junction in Philadelphia, via ex-RDG; to Bison Yard in Buffalo, via ex-EL; and eventually perhaps from Enola to Potomac Yard in Alexandria, Va., should traffic warrant. To operate these routes, D&H would acquire 44 used but mostly choice diesels from LV and RDG, plus twenty new ones from EMD, and approximately 1150 freight cars and cabooses.

Suddenly the D&H had all but doubled itself. This was made possible by a Federal loan extended under the "Three R" Act. On January 26, 1976, $26 million had been approved by USRA, to pay for the purchase of twenty GP39-2's from EMD, acquisition of the Wilkes-Barre Branch, and retirement of existing debt. On March 3 the loan was increased by $2 million to cover the additional extensions in D&H operations that would be formalized a few days afterwards.

April 1, 1976, was "Conveyance Day," when Conrail was officially born of properties legally conveyed to it by its predecessors; when these seven bankrupt carriers then died; and when the D&H extended itself—perhaps overextended itself, as things were to work out. The instant adjustment to new routes, new trains, new men, and new locomotives was a task of monumental proportions, no matter with what apparent confidence Sterzing led the D&H into the fray. But the hard fact of the matter was that the railroad had little choice but to fight in the way it did. To have ventured nothing would have left it bereft of allies, swamped in a sea of Conrail blue. Though not entirely satisfied with all aspects of the extended lines designations, particularly the stringent restrictions on origination and termination of traffic, Sterzing felt that the only hope for D&H lay in acceptance of the expansion, however fraught with uncertainties that course might have been.

In terms of actual operations of trains, what did these expansions mean to the D&H? Flagships of the extended lines were AP-1 and AP-2, the *Apollos,* 100-percent intermodal trains between Oak Island and Chicago via Buffalo inherited from the LV. This six-day-

Apollos *on the extended lines: at Lanesboro (top), Pattenburg Tunnel, N. J. (bottom), and crossing the Delaware River eastbound at Phillipsburg, N. J. (facing page).* KARL R. ZIMMERMANN

710
710

Top: NE-87 emerges from White Haven Tunnel. KARL R. ZIMMERMANN

Bottom: With RS3u No. 504 in the lead, NE-84 heads north out of Allentown Yard. The operator from R Tower waits to hoop up orders. Facing page: AM-1 along the Lehigh River at Jim Thorpe, Pa. ROGER COOK

a-week service operated Oak Island-Dupont via ex-LV Conrail; Dupont-Jefferson Junction, Pa., on the "old" D&H; up the 1.8-mile connection to Lanesboro Junction acquired by D&H in the expansion; to Buffalo via Binghamton and Hornell, N. Y., on ex-EL Conrail; and Buffalo-Chicago as N&W trains. West of Binghamton, *Apollos 3* and *4*—which were Boston trains operating on B&M and D&H—ran combined with *Apollos 1* and *2;* all four trains handled Chicago-bound or -originated TOFC/COFC business exclusively.

The secondary trains in and out of Oak Island were *Mercury 1* and *Mercury 2,* also inherited from the LV. Since D&H was permitted by the USRA agreement to generate only intermodal traffic at Oak Island, the "*Mercs*" were generally short trains across New Jersey, carrying just "pigs" for or from points other than Chicago. Much of the *Merc*'s business came at Bethlehem-Allentown, Pa., where D&H was authorized to interchange with the grandly named Philadelphia, Bethlehem & New England, Bethlehem Steel's switching road. ME-1 and ME-2, the *Mercuries,* were combined west of Binghamton with NE-1 and NE-2, former D&H-EL Mechanicville-Buffalo trains; west of Buffalo, they were handled by N&W. Additional trains to and from Buffalo were AB-91 (Albany-Buffalo) and BM-72 (Buffalo-Mechanicville).

NE-84 and NE-87, the Rigby-"Pot Yard" run-throughs made practical by the Dupont connection, continued as before, but now D&H operated the formerly LV-RDG Dupont-Allentown-Park Junction segment too. For years the best known among D&H freight schedules had been RW-6, called the "Paper Train" for the large quantities of Canadian newsprint it moved south. (Paper has been very important to the D&H; in the early seventies, for instance, it was accounting for as much as one-third of annual revenues.) Originally a Rouses Point-Wilkes-Barre train as the symbol suggested, RW-6 after the extensions operated to Enola via D&H's newly acquired Sunbury line and CR trackage rights, instead of tying up at Hudson Yard near Wilkes-Barre and handing over the tonnage to PC, which had moved it west as train S-81. RW-6 was widely admired among shippers as a "hot" train, both fast and dependable; its northbound counterpart, WR-1, never enjoyed a similar éclat, since it hauled mostly returning empties.

The second pair of trains running north-south on the D&H at the time of the expansion was CX-1 and CX-2, the *Canadian Expediter.* Not long before, this service had had its northern terminal moved from Mechanicville to Rouses Point, its symbols changed

504 504
5005 5005

from AM-1 and MA-2, and its new name coined to lend an aura of urgency. By Conveyance Day it was already an Allentown-Rouses Point run-through over LV and D&H, with power pooling, so "C Day" brought little change, with D&H simply adding LV's mileage to its own.

To keep tabs on this newly expanded empire, the D&H set up the Power Control Center at Colonie, in what once was the crew room and crew caller's office. Two years previous, in the spring of 1974, this building had become the home of the Traffic Control System machines—D&H's version of centralized traffic control. At that time D&H, as an economy measure, had sold The Plaza, its landmark headquarters building in downtown Albany, to the State University of New York and had moved down the block to more modest quarters at 40 Beaver Street. The TCS control boards had been at The Plaza, but D&H's new landlord would not let the railroad bring them to Beaver Street, fearing that the machinery's great weight would be too much for the building. Thus the Traffic Control System found a new home at Colonie; from there a pair of dispatchers control virtually the entire "old" D&H system. The only sections excluded are Oneonta Yard, controlled by FA tower; the Wilkes-Barre area to Carbondale and the Sunbury line, by SX tower at Hudson Yard; and Kenwood (Albany) to Mechanicville, by XO tower there.

Though D&H was among the first railroads to bring virtually its entire system under CTC, the Power Control Center was something new. Reminiscent of PC's huge "Blue Room" in Philadelphia, the D&H center features a schematic map of the railroad, including the extended lines, which covers the room's entire south wall and part of the west. Small magnetized rectangular blocks each bear a train symbol or locomotive or caboose number. The locomotive rectangles may also carry semicircular stick-on tags: red for crippled locomotive, green for one that's due soon for its monthly test, and orange for one due for its annual test. These tags help the power control officers to plan ahead and move the locomotives to inspection points without deadheading.

All locomotives on the roster appear on this huge "game board"—whether stored, in for repairs or test, waiting in an engine terminal, called (or "marked" as they say on the D&H), or on the road. As a train progresses from origin to destination, its blocks are periodically moved across the board to reflect its actual location. Thus the man in charge can see what power he has where and lay his plans

Facing page: Six units power NE-84 north at White Haven. ROGER COOK

Right: An old N&W Geep leads two new D&H ones east across the Delaware River at Phillipsburg with AP-2. The date is March 10, 1976, and the extended operations are in just their second week. MAX ROBIN

The D&H at 3:30 P.M., February 4, 1978.

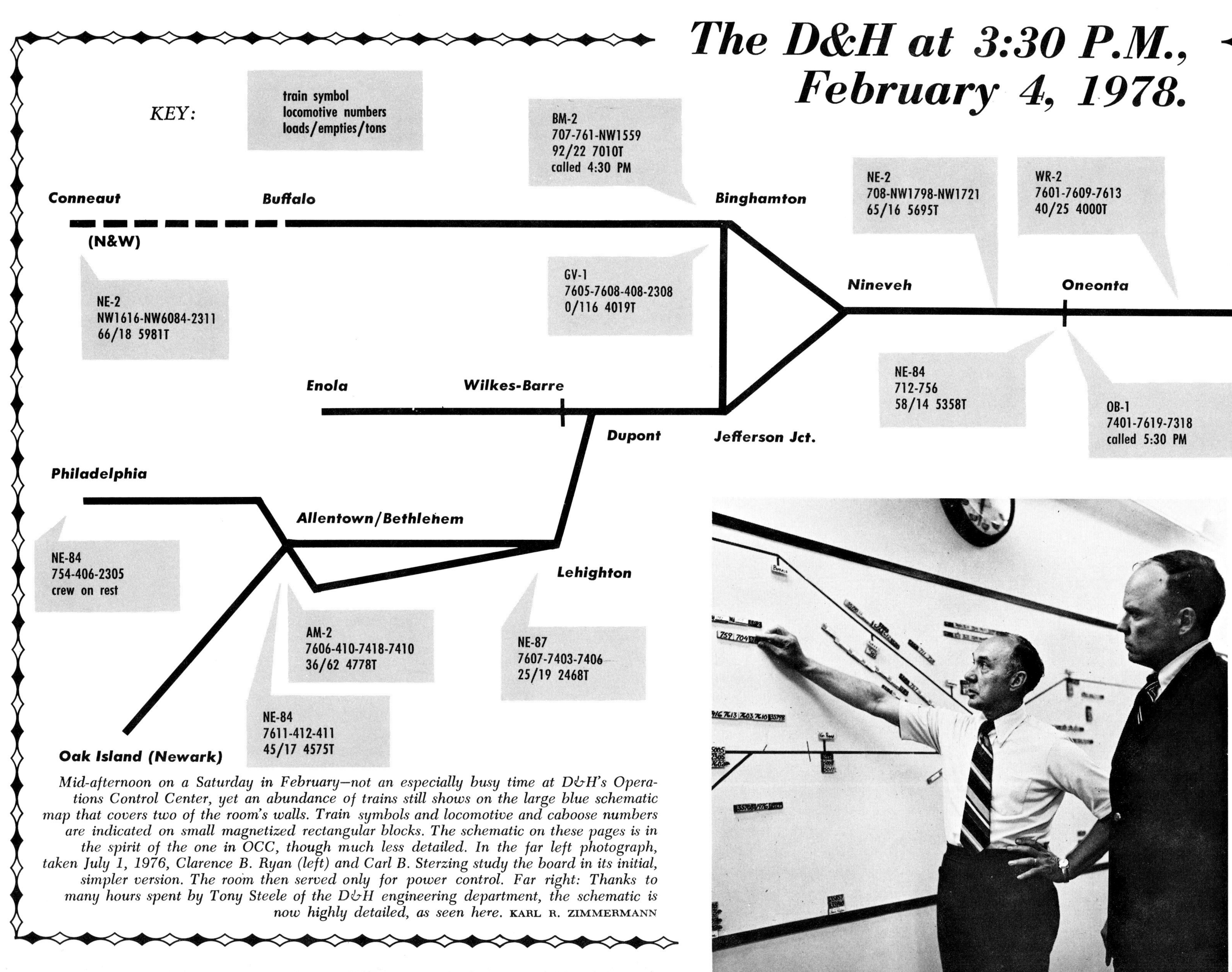

Mid-afternoon on a Saturday in February—not an especially busy time at D&H's Operations Control Center, yet an abundance of trains still shows on the large blue schematic map that covers two of the room's walls. Train symbols and locomotive and caboose numbers are indicated on small magnetized rectangular blocks. The schematic on these pages is in the spirit of the one in OCC, though much less detailed. In the far left photograph, taken July 1, 1976, Clarence B. Ryan (left) and Carl B. Sterzing study the board in its initial, simpler version. The room then served only for power control. Far right: Thanks to many hours spent by Tony Steele of the D&H engineering department, the schematic is now highly detailed, as seen here. KARL R. ZIMMERMANN

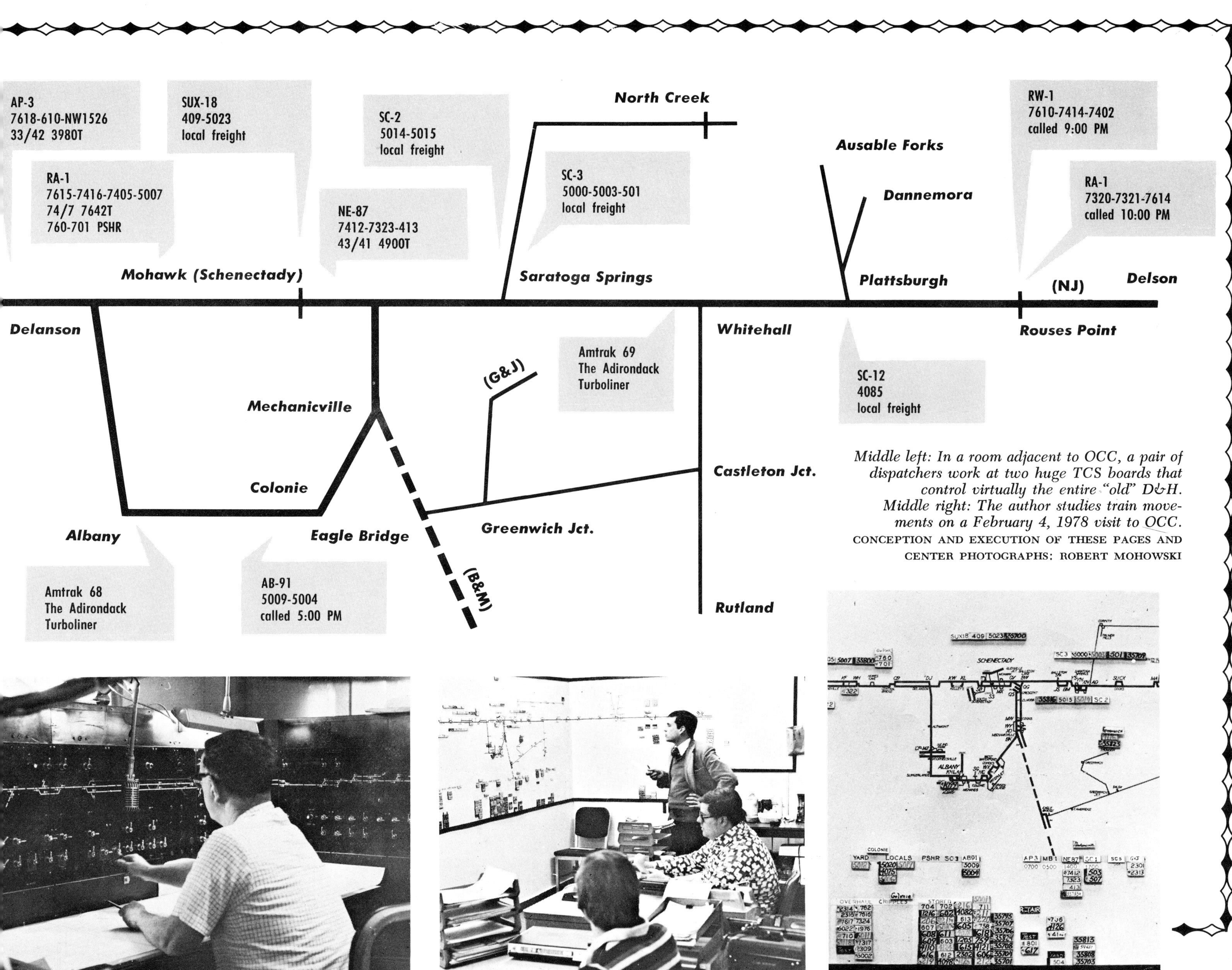

Middle left: In a room adjacent to OCC, a pair of dispatchers work at two huge TCS boards that control virtually the entire "old" D&H. Middle right: The author studies train movements on a February 4, 1978 visit to OCC.

CONCEPTION AND EXECUTION OF THESE PAGES AND CENTER PHOTOGRAPHS: ROBERT MOHOWSKI

accordingly.

Though initially just for power control, in the summer of 1977 the room was upgraded in function to become the Operations Control Center, with a supervisor of sufficient rank to make major decisions on duty at all times. The OCC then became the D&H's nerve center, manned for three tricks by an operations control officer, who is in general charge; a power control officer; and two dispatchers.

A myriad different locomotive numbers have shown up on that power control board since it was instituted in 1976—many of them strange to D&H eyes up till then. For though the D&H diesel fleet was remarkably diverse even before the extensions, it became more so on Conveyance Day.

D&H dieselization had started out on a utilitarian note of standardization. In 1944 the railroad began buying 1000-horsepower S2 yard switchers from Alco-GE; in 1946 it began to order RS2 road-switchers from the same builder. By July 1953, when dieselization was completed, 51 S2's and S4's were on the roster, and 128 RS2's and RS3's—a 100-percent indigenous fleet, all built on-line at Alco's Schenectady works. (In addition, a pair of RS2's had been built by Alco's Canadian subsidiary, Montreal Locomotive Works, Ltd., for D&H's Canadian subsidiary, the Napierville Junction Railway.) For a time, then, the D&H's entire motive power roster consisted of basically only two types of locomotive, and all 181 units wore a solid black paint scheme, enlivened only by yellow safety striping on the locomotives' noses. (As first delivered, they lacked this

Facing page: Alco Centuries lead two lash-ups at Binghamton. Left: At Oneonta, Nos. 5004 and 5005 illustrate the two short hood styles for RS11's and RS36's. Actually, No. 5004 originally had a high hood, which was chopped in 1973 at Colonie; RS11's Nos. 5006-5011 were built with low hoods, as were all twelve RS36's. Below: This lash-up at Allentown shortly after "C Day" shows a variety of power new to the D&H: No. 7611, a GP39-2 that has not yet received D&H shields on its nose and sides; No. 7319, an ex-LV GP38-2; ex-RDG GP39-2 No. 7416; and RS3u No. 508. ROGER COOK

adornment too.) Even *The Laurentian* and other passenger trains were pulled by drab RS2/3's, 21 of which were equipped with steam generators.

After eight years of this aesthetic austerity—which must have been a blow to D&H-watchers, accustomed as they were to the road's abundantly handsome and various steam power—relief arrived in the form of diesels of the second generation. Still faithful to Alco, D&H took delivery of a dozen RS11's in 1961 and a dozen virtually look-alike RS36's in 1963. The first RS11's, Nos. 5000-5005, were high-hood units, and all new. Alco had built them in 1960 "on speculation" for the New York Central. After languishing in NYC's Selkirk Yard for a time without being operated, they were bought by D&H.

The remaining eighteen second-generation RS's had low hoods and were rebuilds of RS3's, under Alco's unit improvement and replacement plan. (RS11 No. 5004 subsequently had its nose chopped at Colonie in October 1973, leaving only five high-hood units.) With these second-generation diesels came the colorful D&H paint scheme of the sixties and seventies: Champlain blue above gray, with a yellow band to separate the two, a plunging blue neckline in front, and D&H shields on nose and cab sides. Eventually the older RS's that remained were put in this scheme too, though no S2's or S4's ever received it.

The next units purchased, in 1964-65, were the monarchs of the roster, at least until the advent of the PA's: eighteen Alco C628's, the handsome and angular "big Centuries," for which another batch

of RS3's were traded in. This ended the era of Alco purchasing by the D&H, since in 1967 the railroad turned to General Electric—one-time Alco partner in the diesel business and also a local firm, headquartered in Schenectady though it built its locomotives in Erie, Pa.—and began buying its U-boats. A dozen U30C's delivered that year were followed by fifteen U23B's in 1969 and nine U33C's in 1970.

If this defection from Alco were not egregious enough—and after all, GE and Alco were near neighbors and nearly siblings, and Alco would soon be defunct as a locomotive builder anyway—what of D&H's brush with EMD in 1967? Impressed by a pair of 3600-horsepower SD45 demonstrators that worked on the D&H system in the fall of that year, the railroad bought them and an additional unit on the spot to meet a power shortage. But these diesels, Nos. 801-803, were clearly strangers in an Alco/GE paradise. In little more than a year they were traded to EL for a trio of U33C's—Nos. 751-753, actually the first three units of that class owned by D&H. This convenience of the Dereco era outlasted the alliance that gave it birth; in fact, it was not until the eve of EL's liquidation into Conrail that the swap was reversed, sending D&H's three ex-EL U-boats to CR and bringing SD45's Nos. 801-803 home to D&H, where they would soon find plenty of fellow EMD units for company.

For on "C Day," D&H entered the EMD camp with a vengeance. It seemed to get the pick of the power from RDG and LV, and that meant Electro-Motive: a dozen GP38-2's from the Valley and twenty GP39-2's from Reading. In addition, twenty new GP39-2's which had been ordered by the D&H in 1975 arrived simultaneously. With impeccable timing, the first of these Geeps worked east on the point of the initial D&H *Apollo 2* on April 1, 1976—Conveyance Day. Nevertheless, casting one look back, D&H also took twelve Alco C420's from LV, thus renewing old ties.

Needed immediately, this newly acquired power was not accorded the honor of a proper cosmetic welcome to the D&H. LV and RDG diamonds were painted out and D&H logos hastily stenciled over top. (Even some of the brand-new GP39-2's went to work bald until Colonie forces had time to apply decals of the D&H shield to the nose and cab.) Since D&H practice is to paint

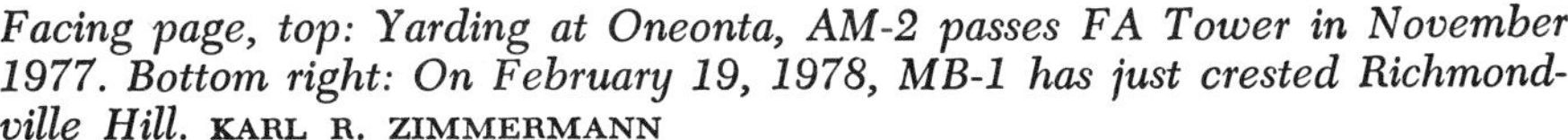

Facing page, top: Yarding at Oneonta, AM-2 passes FA Tower in November 1977. Bottom right: On February 19, 1978, MB-1 has just crested Richmondville Hill. KARL R. ZIMMERMANN

Facing page, bottom: NE-84 near Windsor, N.Y., in the spring of 1974. ROBERT MOHOWSKI

Above: SD45 No. 803 at the summit of Richmondville Hill. When the trio of SD's swapped with EL for U33C's was returned prior to "C Day," D&H simply applied its blue paint over the EL's maroon, yielding a unique livery. Top right: Ex-Reading GP39-2 No. 7418 at Dyes, between Binghamton and Tunnel, with NE-2 in January 1978. ROGER COOK

CHRONOLOGICAL ROSTER OF DIESEL ACQUISITIONS

Class	Road Numbers	Builder	Year Acquired	Notes
S2/S4	3000-3050	Alco-GE	1944-50	1
RS2/RS3	4000-4124	Alco-GE	1946-53	2
RS11	5000-5011	Alco	1961	3
RS36	5012-5023	Alco	1963	
C628	601-618	Alco	1964-65	4
U30C	701-712	GE	1967	
SD45	801-803	EMD	1967	5
PA1	16-19	Alco-GE	1967	6
U23B	2301-2316	GE	1969	7
U33C	751-762	GE	1969-70	5, 8
RF16	1205, 1216	Baldwin	1974	9
RS3	4075, 4082	Alco-GE	1974	10
RS3u	501-508	Alco/M-K	1975-76	11
C420	404-415	Alco	1976	12
GP38-2	7314-7325	EMD	1976	13
GP39-2	7401-7420	EMD	1976	14
	7601-7620	EMD	1976	

NOTES:

1 The last unit in this class was retired in 1970.

2 As of 1/15/78, thirteen units remained on the roster, including No. 4103 (leased to National Lead Industries) and No. 4116 (owned by D&H subsidiary Greenwich & Johnsville).

3 Nos. 5000-5005 were built in 1960 for NYC on speculation and given NYC Nos. 8009-8014, though never officially delivered. Originally all high-hooded, No. 5004 had its nose chopped at Colonie in 1973. Nos. 5006-5011 built with low noses.

4 As of 1/15/78, only Nos. 601, 604, 610, and 617 were in service; the remainder were stored.

5 Former EMD demonstrators Nos. 4354, 4352, 4353, built 1966. In 1969, Nos. 801-803 were traded to EL for U33C's Nos. 3301-3303, which became D&H Nos. 751-753. Units traded back to original owners 4/76.

6 Former ATSF Nos. 59, 60, 62, 66, built 1947-48. Remanufactured by Morrison-Knudsen in 1975 to PA4's. Leased to Massachusetts Bay Transportation Authority 9/30/77.

7 Originally Nos. 301-316; renumbered in 1971 at request of EL. No. 315 wrecked 4/71 and never rebuilt.

8 No. 757 burned and rebuilt at Morrison-Knudsen 10/75; No. 760 wrecked and rebuilt M-K 8/76.

9 Built for NYC in 1951-52 as Nos. 1205 and 1216; later to Monongahela Railway, same numbers; stored 8/1/77; sold 4/1/78 to Castolite (Woodstock, Ill.) for use on the Michigan Northern.

10 B&M Nos. 1508 and 1536, built 1952/54, acquired in trade for D&H Nos. 4075 (first) and 4082 (first) due to need for boiler-equipped power for The Adirondack. Initially carried D&H Nos. 1508 and 1536.

11 Rebuilt at M-K from RS3's Nos. 4106, 4107, 4112, 4113, 4115, 4119, 4122, 4128.

12 Former LV Nos. 404-415, built 1964.

13 Former LV Nos. 314-325, built 1972.

14 Former RDG Nos. 3401-3420, built 1974.

ROSTER DATA: GUS NEGUS, D&H

D&H leased many diesels in recent years. Top: PA's pass a United Railway Supply RS3 at Rouses Point. KARL R. ZIMMERMANN

Middle: StJ&LC Geep at Whitehall in late spring of 1977. ROGER COOK

Bottom: CP RS3 and RS10 southbound out of Port Henry. TOM KELCEC

locomotives only when they are in the shops for major overhaul, and since the Geeps are the newest power the road owns, it's not surprising that all the RDG and LV Geeps ended 1977 in the by-then somewhat tattered dress of their original owners. Six of the LV C420's did receive the traditional D&H blue and gray garb, however: Nos. 404, 406, 408, 410, 411, and 412.

Two directions in future D&H motive power acquisition had become clear by Conveyance Day: locomotives would be EMD and configured B-B, the big C-C diesels proving simply too rough on D&H's curvaceous rails. Meeting half these requirements were the pair of exotics the D&H had acquired back in 1974—"Sharknoses" Nos. 1205 and 1216. They had four-wheel trucks, but they surely weren't Electro-Motive products. Rather, they were Baldwin-Westinghouse RF-16's, built in 1950-51 for New York Central, sold by PC to the Monongahela Railway, and acquired from there by D&H at Bruce Sterzing's instigation for an equivalent weight in scrap metal. The "Sharks"—like the PA's, the last of their kind in the country—arrived at Colonie in August 1974. They were given mechanical attention, including welding of No. 1205's cracked engine block, a repair destined to be endlessly repeated without permanent success; and a blue, yellow, gray, and silver paint scheme modeled on the PA's "warbonnet" styling, which had been inherited from the Santa Fe.

In early 1975 the Sharks entered service. At first they were not allowed to venture very far from the security of the locomotive shops. Briefly they worked transfer runs from Colonie; then they served as pushers on Richmondville Hill and later powered local freights from Whitehall. They finally found a real home on BNW-3 and FO-4, the Binghamton, N. Y.-Sayre, Pa., turn, one of two pairs of trains (the other was LV) that operated pooled service over EL trackage rights and the LV Auburn Branch between these cities. When not on the Sayre turn, the Binghamton-based Sharks were often assigned as Belden Hill pushers.

Then came Conrail, and BNW-3 and FO-4 were no more. On the rebound, the Sharks returned to Whitehall, where they went to work on the local freights on the Rutland Branch, and the Washington Branch to Eagle Bridge, N. Y. The train to Rutland, Vt., known as the "Hill Freight," mostly carried cars for interchange there with the Vermont Railway and the Green Mountain Railroad. The "Slate Picker"—so named when it served the slate quarries in the area, which have been closed for nearly twenty years—ran the same route as the Hill Freight as far as Castleton Junction, N. Y., then headed south toward Eagle Bridge. Its main bit of business was to interchange at Greenwich Junction with the Greenwich & Johnsonville Railway, a D&H subsidiary which operates with an RS3 bought from the parent road. (Later this operation would be changed entirely, with the local job coming out of Mechanicville on the B&M to Eagle Bridge, then heading up the branch to the interchange at Greenwich Junction.)

No matter where they worked, the Sharks had their problems, particularly No. 1205, with the frequently but fruitlessly welded engine block. Sterzing's motivations in their acquisition were the same that had led him to recall the PA's: a sense of the locomotives' worth as "living history"; a desire for the public visibility they might bring, particularly if run on excursions, which they sometimes were; and a hope that they would be a focal point for employee interest and morale. On this last count at least, the Sharks apparently failed. Unlike the PA's, which did capture the imagination of D&H railroaders, the Sharks were as likely to garner contempt as affection. Though crews and shopmen grudgingly admitted that they were powerful brutes which could lug with the best of them at low speeds, they dwelt on the units' extraordinary penchant for breakdowns. Furthermore, hood units provided much better visibility on brush-enclosed branch lines and for switching, so the Sharks were not ideally suited for the service in which they were placed. As the PA's seemed to symbolize the D&H in its time of vigor, the trouble-ridden Sharks came to reflect all too well the state of the railroad as it began to founder. (In 1975, the year when the Sharks arrived, D&H slipped back into the red, with a $1.5 million loss.)

But the Sharks were a near miracle for locomotive buffs, who chased across the system hoping to catch them on a good day, when they were on the road rather than in the shop. While the Sharks were running out of Whitehall and the PA's passing through there in *Adirondack* service, that small town at the southern tip of Lake Champlain became almost a museum for historic diesels. And Sterzing reportedly had tried to get a pair of the last Alco FA's to expand the collection (ex-Spokane, Portland & Seattle units, then owned by Burlington Northern), but the price proved to be too steep.

Top: Sharks leave Whitehall on WR-1 in July 1975; No. 1508, the yard switcher, is a steam-generator-equipped RS3 leased from the B&M. Bottom: The Hill Freight bound for Rutland, at Castleton, Vt., in June 1976. KARL R. ZIMMERMANN

Facing page, top: As Richmondville Hill helpers, Sharks drift downgrade light, returning to Mohawk on May 3, 1975. They broke down and never made it beyond Delanson. ROGER P. COOK

Facing page, bottom: In late July 1975, the Sharks are working FO-4, the D&H half of joint Binghamton-Sayre operations shared with LV. ROBERT MOHOWSKI

If the D&H failed in this particular effort to broaden its collection of unusual and historic diesels, it succeeded on other occasions in creating or importing unique units. Perhaps the most curious of all were the eight RS3's rebuilt at Morrison-Knudsen in 1975 and 1976 with 2000-horsepower 251 Alco engines. Numbered 501 to 508 and designated RS3u's, these *sui generis* units had their noses chopped, in addition to being upgraded and modernized electrically and mechanically. Though chosen for the honor of powering the first westbound D&H *Apollo* on "C Day," with President Sterzing at the throttle for part of the haul, the RS3u's did not prove as reliable as the D&H had hoped.

Earlier, D&H had given M-K some other rebuild business. Best known of course were the four PA1's returned as PA4's, upgraded to 2400 horsepower for use on the *Adirondack*. Shortly after the first two PA's went west for this metamorphosis, they were followed by a pair of damaged U33C's: No. 757, which had burned along with the Binghamton roundhouse in October 1974; and No. 760, which had run away unattended on Ararat and derailed.

After the RS3u's came back from M-K and were evaluated, D&H decided to try some rebuilding on its own at Colonie Shop. Accordingly, a limited pilot program, designed to test the feasibility of doing such work internally, was initiated on April 15, 1976. Under it, one RS11 and six big U-boats received complete "top and bottom" rebuilds, with renewal of engine, trucks, and main generator, complete sandblasting and repainting, and interior cab refinishing. Eight new positions were created at Colonie to do this work, and in addition four men previously doing running repairs were moved over to work on the rebuilding. "Unit exchanging" with GE—that is, pulling out a prime mover and swapping it for a rebuilt one—enabled the work to move forward quickly.

Management was impressed, and began a substantial modernization and rebuilding program on September 1, 1976, projected to continue until June 1978 and encompass thirty units—RS11's and 36's and U30C's and 33C's. Of the $3 million needed to complete the project, one-third was to be paid by D&H and two-thirds by New York State, financed through the same bond issue that made possible *The Adirondack*. This program was to be suspended in the fall of 1977, with only fourteen units completed, by a new management which had set a new direction: toward just a "top deck" rebuild, which is only about half as costly. In this case, the engine is

overhauled and electrical components cleaned and renewed in kind, with none of the modernizing or upgrading of the earlier program. Once completed, a locomotive is good for five and one half years—the D&H maintenance cycle.

To meet its motive power needs in the seventies, D&H leased as well as rebuilt. Units from parent N&W came as early as 1970; in 1975, for instance, a substantial flotilla of N&W U30B's were hauling D&H freight. (N&W units have also showed up on an everyday basis on run-throughs since "C Day.") In addition there were RS3's from CP Rail, United Railway Supply, and B&M (a pair with steam generators, for use on *The Adirondack* while the PA's were in Boise); CP Rail RS10's; nine ex-Long Island Rail Road C420's owned by Rail Traction Corporation; and a pair of St. Johnsbury & Lamoille County GP7's. Adding even more color to the scene were some RS3's leased to the Providence & Worcester and later returned to D&H still wearing P&W orange, brown, and white; and RS3 No. 4098 in Vermont Railway red, sold to that road and later bought back by D&H but not repainted to blue and gray.

To summarize: At some time or other in 1976 or 1977, D&H had on the property Alco PA's, C628's, C420's (both low and high hoods), RS11's and 36's (both low and high hoods), RS10's, RS3's in as many as half-a-dozen paint schemes (if you include subsidiary Greenwich & Johnsonville's unit); GE U23B's, U30C's, and U33C's; EMD GP7's, SD45's, GP38-2's, and G39-2's; and Baldwin RF16 "Sharks." This plethora of different locomotive types must have been somewhat bewildering for the shop forces at Colonie. Providing the final touch of color was a pair of units painted to honor the Bicentennial. U23B No. 2312 was first put in patriotic dress for use on the "Preamble Express" for the *American Freedom Train;* later, without changing colors, she was given D&H markings, renumbered 1776, and named "Spirit of Freedom." She was joined by another celebrant: No. 1976, one of the Morrison-Knudsen RS3u's.

It was appropriate that the D&H join in the Bicentennial festivities, for its rails along Lake Champlain traverse country rich in the heritage of the Revolution. Furthermore, the railroad and its president believed firmly in independence and the American tradition of free-enterprise. However, free-enterprise railroading may have become outmoded in the Northeast, and since Conveyance Day

On June 24, 1976, the Sharks work the Hill Freight: en route from Whitehall to Castleton (facing page, bottom), switching at Castleton (facing page, top), and interchanging with the Green Mountain Railroad at Rutland (above). KARL R. ZIMMERMANN

On a June night in 1975, the Sharks slumber at Colonie, with the first aid so frequently needed close at hand. ROBERT MOHOWSKI

D&H has had increasingly tough going. The reasons for this are various and complex. To begin with, the winter of 1976-77 in the Northeast was the most brutal in memory. This caused an abundance of weather-related accidents and derailments on the D&H, and yards clogged with cars stalled because of rights-of-way made impassable by snow. Then came the spring thaw, bringing floods, ice jams, washouts, and subsequent slow orders. All this led to a greatly decreased level of service and a greatly increased level of expense.

Then there were the extended lines. No railroad can double the scope of its operations overnight and expect all to go smoothly. Though the D&H felt it had had no choice but to accept the challenge of expansion, that path has proved to be rocky indeed. Power often has been in short supply. Though by USRA edict Conrail is required to give D&H trains priority equal to its own, constant vigilance and frequent aggressiveness by the D&H has been needed to see this enforced. Even with everything weighed, the bottom-line figures were discouraging: a $3.6 million loss for 1976, which escalated to over $12 million in 1977.

Clearly all was not well at the D&H, and controversy—quiet at first, later strident—was growing among the factions responsible for the railroad's direction: local D&H management, the N&W, and USRA. Disagreement focused on one issue particularly, the Oak Island piggyback service. Though carloadings on the *Apollo* were adequately high, the trains were apparently unprofitable because of high terminal costs at Oak Island, because discount rates for volume shipment (of ten, thirty, or sixty trailers) cut the profit margin far too fine, and because of the directional imbalance of traffic, which favored eastbound three-to-one for loads. In fact, a survey by an independent consultant indicated that the D&H was losing $3 million a year on its Oak Island piggybackers.

Sterzing was not impressed, feeling the study to be superficial and "a self-fulfilling prophecy." Further, he still hoped to gain access to the lucrative traffic generated by the many refineries in the Newark area, the so-called "Chemical Coast," which had been promised to Chessie had it assumed the competitive role vis-a-vis Conrail that D&H eventually did. By staying in Oak Island, Sterzing thought, the railroad might be able to win its point and be awarded the right to handle this chemical traffic. But some of D&H's top management disagreed, feeling that the *Apollos* should go right away, a sentiment echoed by USRA and N&W.

Left: Running repairs, annual inspections, and even complete rebuilds are carried out in Colonie Shop at Watervliet, N.Y. Above: This sign on the shop is a good example of company pride. KARL R. ZIMMERMANN

Below: The Sharks on a fall 1975 excursion on the Washington Branch. TOM KELCEC

In June of 1977, matters began to come to a head. William E. Ruby had come up from the N&W to take over as vice-president-operations; then, on June 22, USRA exercised its option, written into its agreement with the D&H, to designate a member to sit on the D&H board. It chose Selig Altschul, an airline industry consultant. Subsequently Altschul was named chairman of the three-member board.

USRA had still more leverage to apply—and wasted no time in applying it. D&H's financial position was extremely precarious in that summer of 1977. It had already drawn down $24 million of the $28-million loan, was thus ahead of schedule, and had requested of USRA an additional accelerated drawdown of $2 million. USRA, openly displeased with Sterzing's management of the D&H, dragged its heels. In late July, N&W president John P. Fishwick—once a D&H president himself—suggested that the $2 million drawdown might be essential to save the D&H from bankruptcy. On July 27, Carl B. Sterzing agreed privately to resign. On July 28, the USRA board approved the accelerated loan. On August 1, Sterzing submitted his formal resignation. USRA has claimed that the resignation was not a precondition of the loan, but the timing would seem to belie this.

USRA's position in all this was curious. On the one hand, as D&H's prime banker, with power to grant or deny loans, the government agency had terrible power over the railroad. On the other hand, it was midwife and protector of Conrail, with which Sterzing wanted to remain in head-to-head competition for container and piggyback traffic from Oak Island. It was no wonder that USRA had no use for the scrappy, outspoken Sterzing, who was dedicated to seeing that D&H lost nothing to Conrail without a fight. The wonder was that USRA should be given by circumstance the power to shape the management of a direct competitor to Conrail.

At Sterzing's departure, the D&H board named Altschul, already chairman, to the additional post of chief executive officer, leaving the presidency open. William Ruby and Thomas W. Egan were elevated to senior vice-presidencies in operations and administration respectively, and this troika directed the railroad for a time in what Altschul called "management by objective." Meanwhile Sterzing went to the Chicago, Rock Island & Pacific as general manager.

Altschul's leadership of the D&H proved temporary. On October 31, Charles E. Bertrand was elected president and chief executive

Facing page, top: An RS3u and an RS3 lead the Slatepicker down the Washington Branch. Facing page, bottom: At Greenwich Junction is the interchange with D&H subsidiary Greenwich & Johnsonville. Here the G&J RS3 polls the handsome wood-sheathed buggy from the Slatepicker. ROGER COOK

Above: The D&H's two Bicentennial units make a photo runby at Starrucca Viaduct on a Wilkes-Barre-Oneonta excursion. TOM KELCEC

officer, effective November 16. Bertrand, who began his career in 1937 as a trainman on the Alton, had most recently been vice-president and general manager of Northeast Corridor operations for Amtrak. Previously, he had been president of the Reading for more than a decade. Bertrand was apparently N&W's candidate for the job, and his election brought temporary stability to the management of the D&H. But his sudden death on March 3, 1978, placed the situation back in flux.

What did these cataclysmic leadership changes mean at the grass roots, to those who worked for D&H and those who watched it? For employees, it meant more belt-tightening, reduction in overtime, and some confusion and uncertainty as details of operation changed overnight. For those whose interest in D&H was avocational only—the fans—the alterations were far more devastating.

As soon as it had become known that their patron was resigning, even before the formal date, the Sharks were taken out of service, shoved to the end of a storage track at the Whitehall engine terminal, and left there to languish. Later they were moved to Colonie and put up for sale. The PA's, Sterzing's other prizes, fared better; though they too were withdrawn from freight service, where they'd worked since being bumped from *The Adirondack,* they found yet another life under lease to the Massachusetts Bay Transportation Authority. On the afternoon of September 30, they worked east to Boston from Mechanicville on AP-4, then entered commuter service on the line out of Boston's South Station to Framingham, Mass.

The D&H's big Alco Centuries, surpassed only by the PA's and Sharks in appeal for train-watchers, were also hurried into decline by the Altschul administration. Pro-EMD, pro-four-axle policy had been formulated long before—witness the twenty new GP39-2's ordered back in the fall of 1975—but its accomplishment was made an urgent priority by the new management. Most of the C628's were placed in storage. In October, eight of them were sent to work on the N&W, but a drop in traffic caused by a nationwide coal strike returned them to the D&H in December.

Facing page, left Ex-LV Century 420 No. 408 leads OB-3 downgrade at Hillcrest, N. Y., in October 1977. Facing page, right: Fort Edward children tour the cab of the Bicentennial U-boat. Left: Sterzing's departure is imminent, and accordingly the Sharks and PA's languish out of service at Whitehall. Below: The new order parades at Mechanicville in the form of RS36 No. 5015 in solid blue paint and a Turboliner. ROGER COOK

Those classes of power remaining in service began to receive a new paint scheme, dooming to eventual oblivion the unusually handsome blue, yellow, and gray colors. The new livery is a solid blue, set off by silver trucks, with handrails, pilot plate, D&H shields on nose and cabs, and road name and large numbers on the long hood all in yellow. The first locomotive to be so painted was high-hooded No. 5002, an RS11. "Delaware & Hudson" was rendered on this unit in the script lettering that had been used on the Bicentennials, but block lettering was specified for later repaintings.

The second locomotive to fly the new colors was RS36 No. 5015. Back in September 1972, this unit had been given a never-duplicated experimental scheme—hoods blue, cab and huge "D&H" lettering yellow, trucks, frame, and underbody silver—which it wore until its repainting in 1977 into an even bluer scheme. No. 4075, a boiler-equipped RS3 acquired from the B&M, was next into the new dress, and after that No. 2312, the U23B that had been in Bicentennial colors; other units followed. The motivation for the change in livery was, of course, economy: a saving of $600 per locomotive.

One of Selig Altschul's first official acts as CEO was to cancel an excursion scheduled for October 8 and set future policy against such trips. In a letter to the Mohawk & Hudson Chapter of the National Railway Historical Society, the group sponsoring the trip, Altschul wrote, somewhat ungrammatically: "Our studies show that to run the special passenger trains, while having much to commend themselves to the interested parties in the communities involved, have incurred special problems and costs which have been hurtful to our main operations. . . . I do hope at some future time, should conditions permit, that we can consider resuming these special passenger train excursions."

Some major changes occurred in the freight operations too, most dramatically to the *Apollos*. Even before Sterzing's departure, D&H had attemped to abandon its Oak Island service by assessing an $80 surcharge on each container movement, but the ICC had blocked this maneuver. The road was able to discontinue the discount rates for volume movement, however, and this drove traffic down to the point where, by the end of 1977, just a single train a week, run out of Allentown as a turn, was frequently adequate to handle the traffic.

Schedules systemwide were adjusted for more economical operation and greater efficiency, and some train symbols were changed, bringing them in line with the eastbound-even, westbound-odd convention observed on most railroads. When RW-6 and WR-1 were changed to RW-1 and WR-2, the Paper Train's well-known symbol was lost. CX-1 and CX-2 became RA-1 (Rouses Point-Allentown) and AM-2 (Allentown-Mechanicville); RA-1's Allentown paper business was given a priority equal to RW-1's through the Enola gateway.

Change was the order of the day in the late months of 1977. "You can't take a day off around here," one official said, "or you'll come back and find everything different." In general, the emphasis was on streamlining and centralizing operations. Crews for all but the Penn Division are called from 40 Beaver Street; there is now just a single superintendent for the entire road; the Operations Control Center, now permanently located at Colonie after a brief sojourn at the Albany offices, allows management of all power assignments and train movements from a single room.

One thing that hasn't changed much is the N&W's unwillingness to lend a hand to the D&H in any substantial way. For this reason and others, how the Delaware & Hudson Railway will fare in the future is very much an open question, though the sharply escalating losses in recent years don't provoke much optimism. Bankruptcy and oblivion as part of Conrail are an obvious and ominous possibility. A happier fate might be inclusion with B&M, Maine Central, and Bangor & Aroostook in an all-New England system—Buck Dumaine's old idea, which is still very much alive.

For anyone seeking omens to suggest the D&H's future, the new all-blue diesel paint scheme might not be a bad place to look. The official responsible for devising and choosing this livery vigorously denies that the blue is the same shade Boston & Maine or Conrail uses on its diesels. But the colors are very close, and perhaps the gentleman doth protest too much.

February 20, 1978, in Binghamton, finds the Centuries making their last stand, in pusher service on Belden Hill; RS11 No. 5002, the first unit to have been put into the solid blue livery; and N&W Geeps running through. ROGER COOK